Harrap's Guide to
FAMOUS
LONDON
GRAVES

Harrap's Guide to
FAMOUS LONDON GRAVES

by Conrad Bailey
With a foreword by Sir John Betjeman

Photographs by Philip Sayer

Here halt, I pray you, make a little stay,
O wayfarer, to read what I have writ,
And know by my fate what thy fate shall be.
What thou art now, wayfarer, world-renowned,
I was: what I am now, so shall thou be.

ALCUIN *His Epitaph*

First published in Great Britain 1975
by GEORGE G. HARRAP & CO. LTD
182-184 High Holborn, London WC1V 7AX

© *Conrad Bailey* 1975

ISBN 0 245 52374 X

Composed in IBM Press Roman
Printed and bound
in Great Britain by
REDWOOD BURN LIMITED
Trowbridge and Esher

For Nicholas
and his future heroes
and William for his
encouragement

CONTENTS

The entries are in sections, churches and churchyards, cemeteries and burial grounds, small cemeteries and burial grounds, in order of the pre-1964 boundaries.

CHURCHES AND CHURCHYARDS

CEMETERIES AND GRAVEYARDS

SMALL CEMETERIES AND BURIAL GROUNDS

MAPS AND PLANS

LINE ILLUSTRATIONS

PHOTOGRAPHS

Cover: West Hampstead Cemetery

AUTHOR'S NOTE

To compile a complete guide of all the famous people buried in London would prove to be an impracticable task. So many graveyards and cemeteries have been neglected for years. The private cemeteries have become a liability to their owners, who cannot afford the labour to lay low the undergrowth that threatens to engulf even the larger tombs. Many of the inscriptions have been erased by our inclement weather, so even with a plan and plot number the task of finding a particular grave is daunting. It is only by searching through early guides, biographies and acres of burial grounds, that one can produce a list at all. To the would-be famous grave searcher, I would recommend the early winter or spring — the latter season offers a less sombre setting.

In a few instances there has been a reluctance on the part of private cemetery offices to give information for the compilation of this book; understandably so in cases where vandalism and the cult of black magic have left their corruption. Even so, there is a feeling (and it is not mine alone), that the property speculators are casting their eager eyes over the valuable and desirable landscape perhaps to build more ugly blocks. As cemeteries, they provide open spaces in areas that are already crowded with buildings and roads, and so create havens for the living as well as for the dead. In the nineteenth century they were planned as pleasant diversions, and they contain some great sculptural works by British artists. Unfortunately, today, many of these are badly worn and damaged.

It is interesting to note that Camden's Building Works and Services Committee has recently expressed an interest in Highgate Cemetery with a view to turning part of it into an open space. If they can retain the general character of the original design and not destroy the interesting monumental graves, this could set a pattern for other London councils who may be equally as concerned by the desecration of their burial grounds.

This guide covers an area that is within easy travelling distance from Trafalgar Square and is not intended to be a complete guide to the whole of London.

Lastly, I would like the readers of this book to regard this volume as a tribute to the lives of many of the people therein, and not just a guide to their final resting place.

C.C.M.B.
London 1975

ACKNOWLEDGMENTS

I should like to acknowledge my debt to Sian Foster, who has assisted me in the research and compilation of this book. I am grateful to those who were of assistance at the various churches and cemeteries, especially Norman C. Davidson, Superintendent at St Mary's Roman Catholic Cemetery; Mr Campkin, who is the last of a family of foremen at the Jewish cemeteries; Mr G. Broom and Mr J. H. Powney at West Brompton Cemetery; Mr Skinner, Superintendent at Norwood Cemetery and Mr Malyon at the General Cemetery, Kensal Green. I am grateful for the help of Rosemary Graham and William Bainbridge, who read some of the typescript; also to Linda Freeman, who lent me her eyes and time in exploring the tombstones; to Miss Lesley Young, for her editorial work; Keith Anderson for his assistance in layout and lastly, to Jean Bottali who did a magnificent job in putting my notes into typescript.

C.C.M.B.
London 1975

Maps and Plans by Bill Gardiner
Line drawings by the author

14

FOREWORD

It surprises me that so seemingly strange a book as this has not been published before.

There is a natural hero-worshipping instinct in all of us which likes to see where the remains of those we admired or loved are buried. In London this is not easy because graves of most of the famous who died in London are hidden in one of the huge metropolitan cemeteries which were opened in the last century. The earliest of these, such as Kensal Green, Highgate Old Cemetery and Abney Park had to be within carriage distance of central London. They were an improvement on the city boneyards described by Dickens, or the overcrowded parish graveyard such as that of old St Pancras which Thomas Hardy describes in his poem *The Levelled Churchyard*. Hardy, in his capacity as surveyor in Sir Arthur Blomfield's office, supervized the re-burial of the dead bodies in old St Pancras parish churchyard when the Midland Railway passed through it in the 1860s on the way to its terminus.

The private companies which opened large cemeteries in the 1830s and '40s, though commercial, started with generous instincts. They were to be picturesque parks with curving drives around hillocks topped by Grecian temples and shaded by weeping willows. A meditative walk in a holy Kew Gardens was in the minds of the promoters. The increase of population and shortage of space in these one-time generously laid-out cemeteries has turned them all into forests of weather-stained Carrara marble, stones leaning this way and that, as elder, ash and sycamore thrust saplings through. Only in the layout plans shown in this book can one see the romantic origins of some of the earlier designs. Only in the cemetery office, if it is open, and plans are available, can one trace a grave.

The layout of Kensal Green, with its Greek entrance-gates and mortuary chapels has affinities with John Nash's street and park plans for the Crown Commissioners.

London is short of quiet green spaces and the sort of parks that are not recreation grounds, dedicated to sport chiefly. If we could find the tombs of the famous and even the less famous and leave them with their headstones, there is much to be said for transforming most of London's cemeteries into equivalents of St James's and Green Parks. Whether this is done or not, this book reveals much that nobody knows. The tidy-minded would like to see cemeteries mowed and neatly laid-out in straight rows like a spec. builder's suburb of the 'Twenties. For the romantic there is much to be said for the strange Egyptian columnarium in Highgate Old Cemetery, for the weeds and wild flowers and the foxes' earths and badgers which abound there and, no doubt, in Nunhead and the wilderness of broken stones, brambles and stifled trees glimpsed in Tower Hamlets from the London railway lines to Tilbury and Southend. Perhaps a compromise will be reached as so often successfully happens in England. Perhaps too, this book will inspire another volume on the well laid-out and better maintained Georgian cemeteries of the chief industrial towns, particularly in the North and Scotland.

JOHN BETJEMAN
London 1975

ST HELEN'S CHURCH, BISHOPSGATE

CITY OF LONDON

The City Churchyards and Burial Grounds

'Such strange churchyards hide in the City of London'—Dickens.

There must have been well over a hundred burial sites in the City before the Great Fire. Within its walls there were ninety-seven parishes.

Early remains found on the eastern side of the City near Bishopsgate and Moorfields showed that there were several Roman and Saxon burial grounds. When the foundations of St Paul's Cathedral were being prepared, Christopher Wren found very early graves at different levels. The lowest level contained remains of Romans and Britons who had been buried side by side, proving that they must also have lived together.

In 1940 there were about sixty visible burial sites in the City but today it is difficult to find half that number.

Burial space in the churches was mostly reserved for rich merchants who were benefactors or held a position of some importance in the parish.

During the Great Plague of 1665, the graveyards were soon filled and their levels raised. It is known that some of the smaller graveyards had to be emptied but not what became of the corpses.

Before the Dissolution of the Monasteries, 1536-9, monasteries had their own burial grounds in the City. Burials were made at night after Mass with as little delay as possible. A written absolution was buried with the body.

ALL HALLOWS BY THE TOWER *(or All Hallows, Barking)*

Underground: Tower Hill   Buses: 9a

This was a complete medieval church before it was bombed in 1940. Records for a church on this site go back as far as A.D. 685. It was believed by Stow that Richard I's heart was buried in the old chapel, or beneath the high altar. A banner is said to be buried with it, inscribed:
> *'The old grey church by the Tower Hill*
> *Claims Richard's heart and your good will'.*
It is more likely, in fact, that his heart was buried in the cathedral at Rouen.

GREY, Lord Thomas (d. 1554). The uncle of Lady Jane Grey. He was beheaded in 1554.

HOTHAM, Sir John (d. 1645) and his son, Captain John Hotham (d. 1645). Sir John was Governor of the town of Hull, and, together with his son, shut the gates on King Charles I and declared that they could not open up without orders from Parliament. They were both nevertheless declared traitors and executed for double-dealing by order of Parliament in 1645.

MONMOUTH, Humphrey (d. 1537). Cloth merchant and a great benefactor of the early reformers. He was knighted and served as sheriff in 1535. He sheltered and helped Tyndale and left a bequest for the preaching of reform doctrines.

AUSTIN FRIARS, part of which is the DUTCH CHURCH
(near Throgmorton Street and Old Broad Street)

Underground: Liverpool Street

Buses: 9, 11

This was a medieval foundation, and before it was entirely destroyed, in the Second World War, had parts of the old priory still standing, the nave being used as the church. It was given to Dutch refugees in 1550. The present church was rebuilt in the classical·style.

DE BURGH, Hubert, Earl of Kent (d. 1243). The most powerful subject in Europe at the time of King John and Henry III. Accused of many crimes and imprisoned in the Tower 'bound in chains'. He later escaped and eventually was acquitted and had his earldom restored.

EDWARD (d. 1371). Son of the Black Prince.

FITZALAN, Richard, 3rd Earl of Arundel and Surrey. (1346-97). Beheaded when he quarrelled with John of Gaunt and conspired with the Duke of Gloucester and the Earl of Warwick.

Newgate Street

Underground: St Paul's

CHRIST CHURCH

Buses: 8, 22, 25

This was the site of the conventual church of Grey Friars founded in 1225. Wren built his church here in 1687—only the tower remains. The London Head Office of the Post Office occupies part of this site. Among the burials are:

BAXTER, Richard (1615-91). Presbyterian divine. He was one of the great 'protesters' who sided with Parliament in 1642. He suffered much ill-treatment under Charles II and James II and was imprisoned in 1685-86. His numerous writings include *Reliquae Baxterianae*, 1696.

BEATRICE, Duchess of Brittany (d. 1277). Wife of Richard, Earl of Cornwall and King of the Romans and sister-in-law of Henry III. (Pre-Dissolution)

BOYER, Rev. James (d. 1814). Headmaster of Christ's Hospital at the time when Coleridge and Lamb were students there. Lamb immortalized him in his essay 'Christ's Hospital Five and Thirty Years Ago' from the *Essays of Elia.*

DIGBY, Kenelm (1603-65). Author, naval commander and diplomat. He pleaded Charles I's cause with Pope Innocent X, but quarrelled with him and

returned to England in 1645. He discovered the necessity of oxygen to the life of plants. Also buried here is his wife, Lady Venetia (d. 1633).

GUISCARD, Marquis de (d. 1711). Previously known as Abbé de la Bourlie. A French refugee who stabbed Robert Harley, first Earl of Oxford, in 1711.

ISABELLA of FRANCE (1292-1358). Queen of England. She was the daughter of Philip the Fair of France,who married Edward II of England in 1308. Being badly treated by Edward she returned to France and raised an army with Roger de Mortimer, Earl of March. They invaded England in 1326 and successfully deposed Edward in favour of his son Edward III. Isabella and Mortimer ruled,as regents until 1330 when Edward III had them both arrested and put Mortimer to death for the murder of Edward II in 1327. Isabella retired to a convent until her death.

JOAN OF THE TOWER (1321-62).
Queen of Scotland and youngest daughter of Edward II. While still a child she was married to David Bruce, son of Robert the Bruce, in 1327. She was crowned at Scone in 1331. Her husband was, for a time, a prisoner in England and she was allowed by Edward III to visit him. Later, when her husband became unfaithful, she made her home in England, at Hertford Castle. (Pre-Dissolution)

JOHN, Duc de Bourbon (d. 1443). Taken prisoner at the Battle of Agincourt, 1415. (Pre-Dissolution)

MALORY, Sir Thomas (*fl* 1470) Compiler of *Le Morte d'Arthur*. He translated this from the French into English, twenty-one books in all, which were completed between 1469-70 and printed in 1485 by Caxton.   (Pre-Dissolution)

MARGARET, Queen (*c.* 1282-1318). Edward I's Queen, daughter of Philip III of France. She was his second wife although never crowned, and bore him three children. (Pre-Dissolution)

SHERIFF or SHYRFE, Laurence (d. 1567). London grocer and founder of Rugby School.

WARREN, Baron Sir William and his wife, ISABELLA, Queen of Man. (dates unknown) (Pre-Dissolution)

Minories

Underground: Tower Hill

HOLY TRINITY CHURCH

Buses: 9a

An enclosed order of nuns was founded here in 1293. At the Reformation, the convent became part of the armoury of the Tower of London, and the chapel became the parish church. No trace of the chapel remains today.

ANNE, Duchess of York (1637-71). First wife of James II and mother of Queens, Mary II and Anne. Remains reburied in Westminster Abbey.

LEGGE, George, 1st Baron Dartmouth (1648–91). Son of William Legge, a Royalist. Master of the Horse to the Duke of York, 1673; Governor of the Tower, 1685; Admiral and Commander-in-Chief of the Fleet. He was imprisoned for treason in 1691.

LEGGE, William, 1st Earl of Dartmouth (1672-1750). Son of George Legge (see above). Privy Councillor, Secretary of State and Commissioner of the Board of Trade. He attended Charles I on the scaffold.

Holborn Viaduct

Underground: Chancery Lane

ST ANDREW'S *(Holborn Circus)*

Buses: 8, 22, 25, 501

St Andrew's used to stand at the top of Holborn Hill, but with the construction of the viaduct in 1869 it is now below the level of the main road. The early church goes back to Saxon times. Wren built his church here in 1704. It was completely gutted in one of the 1941 air raids and has now been restored.

Thomas Chatterton's burial record is in the church register, although he was buried in the graveyard of Shoe Lane Workhouse in 1770.

NEELE, Henry (1798-1828). Poet and author who was also a solicitor. Besides his poetry and contributions to periodicals, he also published a *Romance of English History,* 1827. He committed suicide.

SACHEVERELL, Henry (c. 1674-1724). Political preacher of Magdalen College. He also preached at St Paul's. His sermons condemning toleration and promoting non-resistance were published and the House of Commons declared them to be seditious libel. He was later resident preacher at St Andrew's. He died as the result of an accident.

STANTON, Edward (1681-1734). Sculptor. Appointed Mason to Westminster Abbey. Did much work in parish churches. Also his father, William Stanton (1610-74), and his brother, Thomas, known as the 'Holborn Stantons'.

STRUTT, Joseph (1749–1802). Author and artist-engraver whose works include *Chronicle of England*, 1777-78, *Biographical Dictionary of Engravers* and *Sports and Pastimes of the People of England*, 1801. Scott is said to have taken his inspiration for *Waverley* from an idea by Strutt.

TOMKINS, Nathanael (d. 1643). Brother-in-law of Edmund Waller, the poet. He was executed for his share in Waller's plot to secure London for Charles I in 1643.

WRIOTHESLEY, Sir Thomas, 1st Baron Wriothesley of Titchfield and Earl of Southampton (1505-50). Lord Chancellor of England. He was appointed by Henry VIII as one of his executors, and was Privy Councillor to Edward VI. In 1543 he formulated the league between Charles V and Henry which led to the invasion of France in 1544. Together with Warwick he opposed Thomas Seymour, and was in charge of the interrogation of Ann Askew in 1545. Later he was abandoned by Warwick and struck off the list of councillors.

ST ANDREW UNDERSHAFT

(On the corner of St Mary Axe and Leadenhall Street)

Underground: Aldgate

Buses: 15, 25

A church was founded here about the twelfth century, but the present building was erected circa *1532.*

BURTON, Simon (d. 1593). Master of the Company of Waxchandlers and also a governor of St Thomas's Hospital.

CLITHEROW, Sir Christopher (d. 1641). A city merchant of some wealth and importance in his day. Lord Mayor of London in 1635, and Master of the Ironmongers' Company. (Monument in north wall)

DATCHELOR, Mary (d. 1699). Founder of a girls' school in Camberwell. Though called Mrs Datchelor, she was in fact unmarried. (New stone in churchyard. Family vault set behind)

HAMERSLEY, Sir Hugh (1565-1636). Influential city merchant. Lord Mayor in 1627 and President of Christ's Hospital. (Fine monument)

LEVESON, Nicholas (d. 1539). Sheriff of London in 1534. He is buried between the north aisle and the altar with his wife, Dionysia, and family. His wife was the daughter of Thomas Bodley, founder of the Bodleian Library in Oxford.

OFFLEY, Sir Thomas (c. 1505-82). Master of the Merchant Taylors' Company, 1547. Sheriff of London and Lord Mayor in 1556. There is a fine monument by Cornelius Cure, Master-mason to Elizabeth I and James I, and designer of the monument to Mary, Queen of Scots in Westminster Abbey.

STOW, John (c. 1525-1605). Historian. He was also a tailor and a member of the Merchant Taylors' Company. Above the monument is written: *Aut scribenda agere/ Aut legenda scribere* – 'Either do something worth writing about, or write something worth reading about'. The Lord Mayor renews the quill pen in the effigy's hand every year. He collected and transcribed manuscripts and published, among others, *A Survey of London*, 1598. He became destitute towards the end of his life.

Smithfield   **ST BARTHOLOMEW THE GREAT**

Underground: Barbican

The restored Norman church is all that remains of the Augustinian Priory founded by Rahere in 1123. Rahere was buried here in 1144; his tomb is fifteenth-century work by Hubert Le Sueur.

ANTHONY, Dr Francis (1550-1623). Learned physician and chemist. He was frequently fined, also imprisoned by the London College of Physicians, for practising without a licence.

COOKE, Edward (d. 1652). Philosopher and doctor, his tomb was famous because it used to 'weep' – being made of a marble that oozed drops of water in a damp atmosphere. With central heating the tears have dried.

MILDMAY, Sir Walter (c. 1520-89). Founder of Emmanuel College, Cambridge, 1585. Chancellor of the Exchequer, 1566. One of the commissioners presiding at the trial of Mary, Queen of Scots at Fotheringhay Castle in 1587.

RAHERE (d. 1144). He was one of Henry I's courtiers of humble origin who advanced himself through his wit and abilities. After a pilgrimage to Rome he contracted a malarial fever and in his sufferings he declared that if he recovered he would build a hospital for the poor. During a convalescence he saw a vision of himself being cast into a pit and the form of St Bartholomew coming to his rescue. The saint requested that Rahere should found a hospital and a church at 'Smoothfield'. He founded St Bartholomew's Hospital in 1123.

Smithfield   **ST BARTHOLOMEW THE LESS**

Underground: Barbican

The church has the hospital as its parish. There was a chapel here in Rahere's time (d. 1144). Very little of the medieval church survives. George Dance the Younger, 1789, and Thomas Hardwick the Younger, 1825, both restored it. Many of the surgeons and physicians who have worked at the hospital are buried here.

SHIRLEY, John (c. 1366-1456). Writer and transcriber of Chaucer.

WATSON, Thomas (c. 1557-92). Poet. A friend of Sir Francis Walsingham. He wrote many sonnets and was a great Italian and Latin scholar. His work was closely studied by Shakespeare.

WINWOOD, Sir Ralph (c. 1563-1617). Diplomat and Secretary of State. Ambassador to France, 1601-3. M.P. for Buckingham in 1614 and also led the House of Commons in the same year. He helped to secure the release of Raleigh in 1616.

Aldersgate

ST BOTOLPH'S CHURCH *(On the corner of Little Britain)*

Underground: St Paul's

Buses: 6, 8, 22, 25

The present church was built in 1788, after the previous one had been damaged in the Great Fire. The churchyard is now a small park called Postman's Park.

CAVENDISH, Sir William (*c.* 1505-57). Husband of Bess of Hardwick. As an agent for Henry VIII he secured property from monasteries after the Dissolution. Later he returned to Roman Catholicism under Mary.

GILL, Alexander, the Younger (1597-1642). Master of St Paul's school. He was much praised by Milton for his Latin verses,. His ears were cut off because he spoke disrespectfully of Charles I.

RAWLINSON, Thomas (1681-1725). Barrister and book collector. His collection of manuscripts is now in the Bodleian Library. He was satirized by Addison as 'Tom Folio'.

Aldgate

ST BOTOLPH'S CHURCH

Underground: Aldgate High Street

Buses: 10, 25, 78

The first records of a church on this site go back to 1125. In 1741 George Dance the Elder built the present church. The churchyard is small, but interesting features include a tombstone against the wall of the church in memory of Thomas Ebrall, a corn merchant, who was shot by a Life Guardsman in April 1810.

CAREW, Sir Nicholas (*c.* 1490-1539). Master of the Horse to Henry VIII. He was found guilty of treason and beheaded on Tower Hill.

DARCY, Thomas, Baron Darcy (1467-1537). He served under Henry VII and later in France under Henry VIII, but in 1535 fell under suspicion of involvement in a Roman Catholic plot against the King and was beheaded on Tower Hill two years later.

GREY, Henry, Duke of Suffolk (d. 1554). Father of Lady Jane Grey. His severed head was preserved and kept in Holy Trinity Church. Now in this church. He was executed for treason for taking part in Wyatt's rising against the Spanish

Marriage of Mary Tudor.

KENNETT, White (1660-1728). Bishop of Peterborough and chaplain to Queen Anne. He was also a writer and historian— the *Compleat History of England* is his best-known work. He disliked James II's ecclesiastical policies and supported the Puritans.

SYMINGTON, William (1763-1831). Scottish engineer. He took out a patent for an improved form of steam-engine in 1787, and designed the engine for the *Charlotte Dundas*—the first steamboat for practical use—in 1802. This tugboat drew two barges 19½ miles in 6 hours. However, his plans were not supported and he died in poverty.

Bishopsgate ST BOTOLPH'S CHURCH *(near Alderman's Walk)*

Underground: Liverpool Street   Buses: 6, 8, 22

The present church was built in 1728. Although the old church escaped the Great Fire, it had become so ruinous that it had to be replaced. Several Roman remains and skeletons were found during the present church's construction. In the burial ground attached to the church was buried the famous Puritan, John Lilburne, who died in 1657.

BLIZZARD, Sir William (1743-1835). Twice President of the Royal College of Surgeons. F.R.S., 1787.

GOSSON, Stephen (1554-1624). Rector of the church and author of *School of Abuse,* 1579. This was dedicated, without authority, to Sir Philip Sidney, and occasioned Sidney's *Apologie for Poetrie,* published 1595.

JONSON (d. 1600). Ben Jonson's infant son.

PINDAR, Sir Paul (*c.* 1565-1650). Diplomatist and prosperous merchant who also was a great benefactor of the church. He gave most of his money to help Charles I, and also contributed to the restoration of old St Paul's. His house-front was preserved and is in the Victoria and Albert Museum.

RILEY or RYLEY, John (1646-91). Portrait painter. Painted portraits of Charles II and James II and their Queens. Court painter to William and Mary.

Fleet Street   ST BRIDE'S

Underground: Temple   Buses: 6, 9, 9a, 11, 15

The first church here dated from the thirteenth century, but was rebuilt by Wren in 1680. It had the highest Wren steeple. The present church was restored after being gutted in the Second World War. Until the last century the church was called St Bridget's, and the old well is said to be beneath the church. Among those buried in the churchyard, which was on the south side, were Wynkyn de Worde and Thomas Sackvill

BAKER, Sir Richard (1568-1645). Religious and historical writer. He died in the Fleet Prison, where he was held for debt, 1635-45. (Old church)

DAVENANT, Charles (1656-1714). Political economist and writer. He attacked the clergy in his work, *Essays upon the Balance of Power,* 1701.

FLATMAN, Thomas (1637-88). Poet and miniature painter.

FRITH, Mary (1584-1659). 'Moll Cutpurse'—a notorious pickpocket, fortune-teller and forger. She did penance at Paul's Cross in 1612.

LLOYD, Robert (1733-64). Poet and editor of the *St James's Magazine.* His comic opera, *The Capricious Lovers,* was performed in 1764. He was a friend of Garrick, Churchill and Wilkes. Imprisoned for debt.

LOVELACE, Richard (1618-58). Poet and cavalier. He wrote the famous line 'Stone walls do not a prison make', while imprisoned in 1642 for support of the Kentish Petition. He was imprisoned again in 1648, and during this period he prepared his *Lucasta: Epodes, Odes, Sonnets, Songs Etc.,* published in 1649.

MONCKTON, Mary, Countess of Cork and Orrery (1746-1840). She was known as a 'blue-stocking' and entertained many notable people, including the Prince Regent, Byron, Sheridan and Scott. Dickens is said to have portrayed her as Mrs Leo Hunter in *Pickwick Papers*.

OGILBY, John (1600-76). Author and printer. In early life he taught dancing and became master of the revels, but later set up a large printing house and published verse translations of Homer, Virgil and Aesop's *Fables*. His house and books were destroyed in the Great Fire of London in 1666.

RICHARDSON, Samuel (1689-1761). Novelist. He started in business as a printer in Fleet Street. His first novel, *Pamela*, was published in 1740 and was translated into French and Dutch. He won fame in Europe with his novel *Clarissa Harlowe*, 1740. Also buried here are his two wives, Martha *née* Wilde (d. 1730-1) and Elizabeth *née* Leake (d. 1773) and two of his sons.

SACKVILLE, Thomas, 1st Earl of Dorset (1536-1608). Barrister, writer and also a commissioner at State trials. Grand Master of the Order of Freemasons, 1561-70. He announced to Mary, Queen of Scots, her sentence of death in 1586. His poetical works were published in 1859.

SANDFORD, Francis (1630-94). Herald; Rouge Dragon Pursuivant, College of Arms, 1661. Author of *Genealogical History of the Kings of England* 1677. He was confined to Newgate Prison for debt, and died there.

WORDE, Wynkyn de (d. 1534). Printer and stationer. He was born in Alsace (real name Jan von Wynkyn). When he came to England, he became apprenticed to Caxton, whose business he carried on after the latter's death. He opened his own shop in St Paul's churchyard in 1509, and printed, among other works *Morte d'Arthur*, 1498 (2nd ed.) and the *Canterbury Tales*. (3rd ed.)

St Dunstan's Hill   ST DUNSTAN IN THE EAST

Underground: Monument   Buses: 9a

Wren rebuilt the church after the Great Fire. The body of the church was removed in 1817 and replaced, but this section was then destroyed in the Second World War. Wren's tower still stands today, the spire supported by flying buttresses. The church is now a City open space.

BACON, James (d. *circa* 1573). Alderman, fishmonger and sheriff.

Fleet Street   ST DUNSTAN IN THE WEST

Underground: Temple   Buses: 6, 9, 9a, 11, 15

The present church was built in 1831 on the site of an earlier, thirteenth-century church. The old churchyard was surrounded by booksellers' shops. William Tyndale, the translator of the New Testament, *was vicar here, 1528-36. Among those buried in the old church was Thomas Campion, the poet.*

CALVERT, George, 1st Baron Baltimore (*c.* 1580-1632). Statesman. Secretary to Sir Robert Cecil and M.P. for Yorkshire in 1621. He founded a colony, Avalon, in Newfoundland in 1621-23, but was prevented by the Virginia Company from founding another colony south of the James river.

CAMPION, Thomas (d. 1619). Poet, musician and physician. He published Latin verses in 1595 and produced masques for the Court.

FARR, James (d. 1681). Proprietor of the Rainbow Tavern, 15, Fleet Street.

FISH, Simon (d. 1531). Theologian and pamphleteer. He was one of the circle of young men who gave expression to the dislike of Wolsey and denounced the riches of the Church. Fearing the wrath of Wolsey, he fled to the Netherlands where he met other English exiles, Tyndale and Roy, and worked towards the Reformation in England. He later returned to England to promote Tyndale's *New Testament,* and was the author of *Supplication of the Beggars,* which expressed humorously the discontent of the people with the Church.

GRINSELL, Thomas (d. 1645). The man to whom Izaak Walton was apprenticed. (Probably the same as a Thomas Grinsell,

member of the Ironmongers' Company who married Walton's sister Anne.)

MARSHALL, Joshua (1629-78). Sculptor and master-mason. He worked on City churches after the Great Fire. His work can be seen at Chipping Campden, Gloucestershire and East Carlton, Northamptonshire.

MUDGE, Thomas (1717-94). Horologist. Watch-maker to the King, and constructor of elaborate chronometers. He made many improvements to the maritime chronometer and won an award for his first chronometer of this type, 1792.

PINCHBECK, Christopher (*c.* 1670-1732). Clockmaker and inventor of the copper and zinc alloy which bears his name. Anything made in this metal at that period is now very valuable.

WADLOE, Simon (d. 1627). Landlord of the Devil Tavern in Jonson's time.

WALTON, Rachel *née* Floud (d. 1640). Wife of Izaak Walton.

Lombard Street   ST EDMUND THE KING AND MARTYR

Underground: Bank   Buses: 8, 15, 22, 25

This Wren church was built in 1670 on the site of an earlier church, destroyed in the Great Fire. The area was originally a grass market.

MILLES, Dr Jeremiah F.R.S. (1714-84). Dean of Exeter. Took a great interest in archaeology and was President of the Society of Antiquaries from 1768 until his death. He was also a member of the Egyptian Club.

SHUTE, John (d. 1570). Published one of the earliest English books on architecture, *The First and Chief Groundes of Architecture,* 1563.

Cripplegate   ST GILES CHURCH *(Fore Street, Barbican)*

Underground: Moorgate   Buses: 4, 141, 502

The first church was probably built during the reign of Canute. It survived the Great Fire but was completely burnt out in the Second World War. It was entirely restored and reopened in 1960. This parish was the worst hit by the Great Plague of 1665, apparently because the parish water-pump was in the churchyard. About 8 000 died of the plague in one year.

ASTON, Anne. A daughter of Sir Thomas Lucy (see below), the owner of Charlecote, Warwickshire. One of his grand-daughters is also buried here.

BULLEIN, William (d. 1576). Physician. Rector of Blaxhall, Suffolk, but resident in London. One of the earliest British herbalists and author of *A Dialogue against the Fever Pestilence,* 1564.

FOXE, John (1516-87). Martyrologist. Born in Boston, Lincolnshire. He was made a fellow of Magdalen College, Oxford, in 1539, but resigned his fellowship in 1545 because he was unwilling to conform to the religious statutes of the time. His *A Sermon on Christ Crucified* was published and reprinted many times. He attended his former pupil, the Duke of Norfolk, at his execution in 1572. Author of *The Book of Martyrs.*

FROBISHER, Martin (*c.*1535-94). Navigator. He made his first voyage to Guinea in 1554 having acquired his seamanship on expeditions to Africa. In 1566 he was called to account on suspicion of having fitted out his ship as a pirate vessel. He voyaged in search of the North-west Passage and gave his name to Frobisher Bay, 1576. He commanded the *Triumph* in the battle with the Armada and later died of wounds received in a fight while leading his men ashore at Brest.

LUCY, Sir Thomas (1532-1600). Owner of the great estate of Charlecote, Warwickshire, he rebuilt the manor house there in 1558. He was alleged to have prosecuted Shakespeare for deerstealing on his estate in 1585, and is said to be portrayed as Justice Shallow in *Henry IV.* He was greatly influenced by John Foxe, the martyrologist (see above), whose Puritan principles he adopted.

MILTON, John (1608-74). Poet. He was educated at St Paul's School and Christ's College, Cambridge, and lived at Horton. He wrote *L'Allegro, Il Penseroso* and *Comus* during the period 1632-34. In 1643 he married Mary Powell, who left him after a month. At this time he made himself notorious for his pamphlet on the *Doctrine and Discipline of Divorce.* He was reconciled with his wife in 1645. In 1654 Milton became blind and also married his second wife, Catherine Woodcock, who died in 1658. Milton was arrested for his anti-Restoration views, but was released and fined. He married his third wife, Elizabeth Minshull, in 1662. *Paradise Lost* was finished about 1663, and sold 1 300 copies by 1688. Milton's last poems, *Paradise Regained* and *Samson Agonistes,* were published in 1671. He died of gout. Also buried here is Milton's father, John, who died in 1647.

SMITH or SMYTH, Richard (1590-1675). Book collector. He formed a very valuable library at Little Moorfields and was well-known as the compiler of the *Obituary of Richard Smyth . . . 1627-74.*

SPEED, John (*c.* 1552-1629). Historian and cartographer. His first job was as a tailor in his father's business. In 1598 he was working in Custom House as a mapmaker. Author of a *History of Great Britaine,* 1611. (Monument)

WELBY, Henry (d. 1636). Eccentric and hermit. He entered St John's College, Cambridge in 1558, but later, in 1592, became a recluse and lived in Grub Street, giving all his money to charity. This was said to be out of mortification for his brother John's violent character. His biography, published in 1637 after his death, calls him 'The Phoenix of these late Times'.

Underground: Liverpool Street   Buses: 6, 8, 22

The church occupies the site of early Roman buildings and has a Saxon foundation. The present church is pre-Great Fire. It was founded circa 1210, although most of the building is fifteenth-century. It was built as a parish church and had a Benedictine convent added to its north side, the nave on the south remaining parochial. It has a fine collection of tombs, eighteen of them having been removed from St Martin Outwich.

ADELMARE, Sir Julius Caesar (d. 1636). Master of the Rolls and Privy Counsellor to James I. His tomb shows a deed with the seal broken off—a promise to pay the debt of nature as soon as it pleases God. His travelling library is in the British Museum. (In nuns' choir)

BANCROFT, Francis (d. 1727). Founder of Bancroft's School and of the Drapers' Company charity. (In nuns' choir)

CROSBY, Sir John (d. 1475). Alderman and great merchant of London. Sheriff, 1470, diplomatic agent and Mayor of the Staple of Calais. He built the great Crosby Mansion in Crosby Place, now removed to Chelsea. Left alms for St Helen's Church. (In south transept)

GENTILI, Alberico (1552-1608). Italian jurist and Regius Professor of Civil Law at Oxford, who was forced to leave Italy as a heretic. Permanent Advocate for the King of Spain, 1605.

GODDARD, Jonathan (1617-75). Gresham Professor of Physics, 1665. Physician to Oliver Cromwell. He is supposed to have been the first English-man to make telescopes. (In chancel)

GRESHAM, Sir Thomas (c. 1519-79). Founder of the Royal Exchange, 1566-8, and Gresham College. He was appointed by Elizabeth I as Royal Agent at Antwerp in 1552. One of London's most famous citizens. (In nuns' choir)

HOOKE, Robert (1635-1703). Philosopher, mathematician and inventor. He assisted Robert Boyle with his air pump, and Newton in optics. He was Curator of Experiments to the Royal Society, 1662, and Professor of Geometry at Gresham. He noted the real nature of combustion, discovered the fifth star in Orion, 1664, and first asserted the true principle of the arch. He expounded the true theory of elasticity and kinetic hypothesis of gases in 1678, and invented many instruments—e.g. marine barometer. (In chancel)

PICKERING, Sir William (1516-75). Ambassador in France in 1551. He opposed the Spanish Marriage and was involved in Wyatt's conspiracy, although later pardoned, and became Ambassador in Spain under Elizabeth I.

Sir William Pickering

ST KATHERINE CREE

Underground: Aldgate   Buses: 15, 25

There was an earlier church built here circa 1300. The present church was built on the site of the cemetery of Holy Trinity Priory in 1631, and was one of the Laud churches. (Attributed to Inigo Jones)

GAYER, Sir John (d. 1649). Lord Mayor in 1646. A follower of Charles I, he was imprisoned by Parliament. He was a Warden of the Fishmonger's Company and a Director of the East India Company. Whilst trading in the Levant, he once came face to face with a lion. Being a pious man, he dropped to his knees and remained motionless in prayer, so that the lion left him alone. In his will he left a sum of money for a sermon to be preached, annually, on the date of his meeting with the lion.

HOLBEIN, Hans, the Younger (1497-1543). Painter to Henry VIII. He died in the house of Sir Thomas Audley, in Mitre Square, in 1543 of an epidemic illness, and is thought to have been buried here. He made portraits of Erasmus, Thomas More and Henry VIII.

THROGMORTON, Sir Nicholas (1515-71). Chamberlain of England and Ambassador to France. During Queen Mary's reign he found favour despite his connection with Lady Jane Grey. He was later tried and acquitted for his part in Wyatt's rebellion. He was a personal friend of Mary, Queen of Scots, and supported her claim to the English Throne. Throgmorton Street, London EC2, was named after him.

Gresham Street   ST LAWRENCE JEWRY

Underground: Bank or St Paul's   Buses: 8, 22, 25, 501

There has been a church here since the end of the twelfth century. The name Jewry came from the Jewish community which lived here before being expelled by Edward I. The present church, built by Wren and said to have cost more than any other Wren City church, was gutted by fire in 1940 and has since been restored. Sir Thomas More preached here at the beginning of his career.

TILLOTSON, John, Archbishop (1630-94). He was, at first, a Presbyterian, but accepted the Act of Uniformity, becoming Dean of St Paul's in 1689, and Archbishop of Canterbury in 1691. He was famed for his tolerance and also for his brilliant polemical sermons. Author of the *Rule of Faith* and the *Socinians.* He was a lifelong friend of John Wilkins (see below) and married his stepdaughter, Elizabeth French (Cromwell's niece)

WILKINS, Dr John (1614-72). One-time Vicar of St Lawrence Jewry. He was educated at Oxford, where he was later made Warden of Wadham College, and then became Master of Trinity College, Cambridge. In 1668 he was made Bishop of Chester. He was well-known for his tolerance and moderation, but was also accused of lack of principles because he was at peace with both Cromwell and the Royalists—in fact he married Cromwell's sister, Robina. Founder member and first Secretary of the Royal Society. Published, among others, *The Discovery of a World in the Moone,* 1638 and *A Discourse tending to prove that 'tis probable our Earth is one of the Planets,* 1640.

Lower Thames Street   ST MAGNUS THE MARTYR

A church was founded here before the Conquest. A later one was among the first of the churches to be burnt in the Great Fire. The present church was built by Wren in 1676.

COVERDALE, Miles (1488-1568). Rector of St Magnus and one-time Bishop of Exeter. He translated the Bible into English (first edition published in 1535) and also edited the 'Great Bible', 1539, and Cranmer's Bible, 1540. He was buried in St Bartholomew's—'by-the-Exchange', but his remains were later removed to St Magnus.

LAWSON, Admiral Sir John (d. 1665). Anabaptist and republican, who was arrested and accused of involvement in the conspiracy of the Fifth Monarchy Men, 1657. He was Vice-admiral of the Red Squadron against the Dutch, 1665, and died of a wound received in action.

YEVELE, Henry de (c. 1320-1400). Master-mason to Edward III, Richard II and Henry IV. Architect of Canterbury Cathedral, Westminster Abbey naves and Westminster Hall.

Fenchurch Street
ST MARGARET PATTENS CHURCH *(Rood Lane)*

The church was built by Wren, in 1687, on the site of an earlier church, which was burnt in the Great Fire.

BIRCH, Dr Thomas (1705-66). Historian and biographer. His works, though detailed and accurate, are considered very dull. He became Rector of St Margaret Pattens in 1746 and was buried in the chancel there when he died. One-time Secretary of the Royal Society.

Queen Victoria Street
ST MARY ALDERMARY *(Between Watling Street and Bow Lane)*

An early church was founded here, probably before the Conquest. A church that was erected in 1511 was burnt in the Great Fire. Wren built the present one, 1681-2.

CHAUCER, Richard (c. 1348) (according to Stow). Step-grandfather of Geoffrey Chaucer, the first great English vernacular poet.

POTT, Percivall (1714-88). Surgeon. He was in charge of surgery at St Bartholomew's Hospital, London, and introduced many improvements in the art of surgery. He suffered a fracture of the leg in 1756 (a compound fracture still known as 'Pott's Fracture'), and other surgeons were in favour of amputation, but he and a colleague, Nourse, succeeded in repairing the fracture without resorting to this. The spinal disease known as 'Pott's Disease' was so named after his published discussion on this disease in 1779.

Aldermanbury
ST MARY THE VIRGIN *(On the corner of Love Lane)*

Underground: St Paul's or Moorgate   Buses: 8, 22, 25, 501, 502

A fifteenth-century church on this site was burnt down in the Great Fire. This was replaced by Wren's church, which was burnt in 1940. The remains were later shipped to Westminster College, Fulton, USA, to be erected there as a memorial to Winston Churchill. The old churchyard is next to a garden.

CALAMY, Edmund (1600-66). Co Author of *Smectymnuus*. He was a Presbyterian curate at the church, 1639-62, but was ejected after the Act of Uniformity, 1662. He opposed the execution of Charles I and was imprisoned for preaching without a licence. (Buried under the pulpit of the old church)

CONDELL, Henry (d. 1627). Actor at the Globe and Blackfriars Theatres.

HEMMINGE, John (*c.* 1556-1630). Chief proprietor, with Burbage, Condell and Shakespeare, of the Globe Theatre. A fellow actor of Shakespeare, and editor with Condell of the First Folio of Shakespeare's plays, 1623.

JEFFREYS, George, Judge (1648-89). He died in the Tower and was buried here, but there was no trace of his coffin when the church underwent restoration. He was notorious for his brutality, especially at the 'Bloody Assizes', 1685, after the Monmouth rebellion.

SMITH, Lieutenant John (d. 1782). Drowned off Staten Island, New York.

Cannon Street
ST MICHAEL PATERNOSTER ROYAL *(College Hill)*

Underground: Mansion House or Cannon Street   Buses: 9a, 513

The name 'Royal' may originate from the district inhabited by merchants who imported wines from La Réole near Bordeaux. The church was first mentioned in the thirteenth century. It was rebuilt by Dick Whittington, who was buried here, according to his wish. The medieval church was burnt in the Great Fire and was reconstructed by Wren in 1713. This church, in turn, was hit by a flying bomb in 1944, but has now been restored. Burials were in the pre-Fire church.

CLEVELAND, John (1613-58). Cavalier, poet and satirist. He was imprisoned at Yarmouth in 1655, but released by Cromwell. He published his *Poems* in 1656.

WHITTINGTON, Richard (*c.* 1358-1423). Three times Lord Mayor of London. Son of Sir William Whittington, a mercer in London who was also Mayor of London and an alderman. He was a very wealthy man who made loans to Richard II, Henry IV and Henry V. Also a great benefactor, founding a college and an almshouse. His remains were disinterred and reburied twice. The popular legend of Dick Whittington and his cat was not known before 1605, when the ballad was published.

Cornhill

ST MICHAEL'S CHURCH

There has been a church here since the twelfth century. The present church was built by Wren, with a tower by Hawksmoor. The churchyard garden is on the medieval cloister site.

FABYAN, Robert (d. 1513). Sheriff of London in 1493. He held Newgate and Ludgate against the Cornish rebels in 1498. He was the author of the chronicles from the arrival of Brutus in England, to the death of Henry VII, first printed in 1516, *The Concordance of Histories.*

STOW, Thomas (d. 1559). A tallow-chandler and father of John Stow, chronicler and antiquary. Also John's grandfather Thomas (d. 1527) buried at St Michael's near the church walls. Also buried here are the grandfather and great-grandfather of John Stow.

King William Street   ST MICHAEL'S *(Crooked Lane)*

An early church on this site goes back to about the thirteenth century. The Wren church was demolished in 1831 for city development. Coffins from the burial ground were re-interred in the churchyard of St Martin Orgar (now a private garden).

WALWORTH, Sir William (d. 1385). A wealthy London merchant who was Lord Mayor of London in 1374. He is chiefly remembered for his part in quelling the Kentish peasants' revolt of 1381, when he held London Bridge against the peasants and later stabbed and killed Wat Tyler in

front of King Richard II at Smithfield. He was an eminent member of the Fishmongers' Company, and there is a statue of him in the Fishmongers' Hall. A figure of him was displayed in the mayoral pageant of 1616 and 1799.

Hart Street   ST OLAVE'S

The church was built by Robert Cely (according to Stow) in the fifteenth century, but the crypt dates from the thirteenth century. It was gutted in 1941 and rebuilt. The churchyard was used for burials during the Great Plague and skulls over the gateway in Seething Lane commemorate this. The church is known as the parish church of Samuel Pepys, and the position of his pew in the gallery is marked.

PEPYS, Samuel (1633-1703). Diarist. He was educated at St Paul's School and at Trinity Hall and Magdalene College, Cambridge. He was Clerk of the King's Ships and Clerk of the Privy Seal in 1660, remaining at his post throughout the

Plague of 1666, and until 1679, when he was deprived of his offices and sent to the Tower on a charge of complicity in the Popish Plot. However, he was later released and became Secretary to the Admiralty. His famous diary remained

in cipher at Magdalene College until 1825.
Fifty volumes of his manuscripts are in
the Bodleian Library, Oxford. After his
retirement he lived for some years in
Clapham.
Also buried here is his wife, Elizabeth St
Michel, who died in 1669 at the age of
twenty-nine. She was married to Pepys
when she was only 15 years old.
(Buried beneath the high altar in vaults)

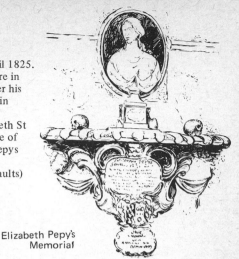

Elizabeth Pepy's
Memorial

ST PAUL'S CATHEDRAL

Underground: St Paul's   Buses: 6, 8, 11, 15, 22, 25

*St Paul's Cathedral is the fifth church to be built on this site, the first having been built
by the Christians at the time of the Roman occupation. The foundation of Wren's
Cathedral was laid in 1675, but the building was not completed until 1710.
Formerly the churchyard extended over a much wider area and had six gates, the main
one being at Ludgate Hill. In the sixteenth century several executions took place here,
including that of Henry Garnett, the Jesuit involved in the Gunpowder Plot. Until the
Great Fire of 1666, many booksellers lived and carried on their business in the churchyard. However, the whole area was cleared to make way for the Cathedral. Amongst
those buried in old St Paul's were:*

BACON, Sir Nicholas (d. 1579). Lord
Keeper of the Great Seal, 1558. He was
one of Elizabeth I's counsellors.

CONSTANCE of Castile (d. 1394). Second
wife of John of Gaunt.

DONNE, John (1573-1631). Dean of St
Paul's and metaphysical poet. He was
converted from Roman Catholicism and
became one of the most famous preachers
of his day.

ETHELRED II (c. 968-1016). King of
England. He is commonly known as 'the
unready', but in fact the name given to

him was *rāedlēas* meaning 'without
counsel'.

JOHN of GAUNT (1340-99). Duke of
Lancaster and uncle to Richard II. He
fought campaigns abroad with his brother,
the Black Prince, and later supported and
influenced Richard, which made him
unpopular.

LILY, William (c. 1468-1522). High-
master of St Paul's School. He was a
grammarian and classical scholar.

LINACRE, Thomas (c. 1460-1524).
The founder of the Royal College of

Physicians and tutor in Greek to Thomas More and Erasmus.

SEBBA (d. *circa* A.D. 695). King of Essex.

SIDNEY, Sir Philip (1554-86). Poet, Court favourite and Ambassador of Queen Elizabeth I. His best known work is *Arcadia*.

VAN DYCK, Sir Anthony (1559-1641). A Flemish artist who became Court painter to Charles I. He was one of the best portrait painters of his day.

The following are buried in the crypt:

ALMA-TADEMA, Sir Lawrence, O.M., R.A. (1836-1912). Painter. He was born in Holland and studied at Antwerp under Hendrik Leys, but made his home in England in 1869 and became naturalized in 1873. He devoted much time to the study of the life of the Romans and Greeks.

ATTWOOD, Thomas (1765-1838). Musician and pupil of Mozart. Son of a coal merchant. After studying in Naples and Vienna, he was appointed Organist to St Paul's and the Chapel Royal, and was the author of several anthems for royal occasions. Died at Cheyne Walk.

BARRY, James (1741-1806). Irish painter, born in Cork. He studied art in Dublin and in Italy. Whilst Professor at the Royal Academy, he launched an attack against its policies and was expelled in 1799.

BEATTY, David, 1st Earl of the North Sea and Brooksby (1871-1936). Admiral of the Fleet, 1919, and First Sea Lord, 1919-27. He commanded a battle cruiser squadron in the First World War and took part in the Battle of Jutland, 1916. He attended the conference on arms limitation in Washington, 1921.

BEERBOHM, Sir Max (1872-1956). Originally Henry Maximilian. Caricaturist and writer of satire. He was most famous

for his subtle caricatures of politicians and intellectuals and was dramatic critic for many years of the *Saturday Review*.

BOYCE, William (1710-79). Composer. He was educated at St Paul's School, where he was a chorister. Later he was Organist to the Chapel Royal. He wrote music for the theatre and the church.

CARNEGIE, William, 7th Earl of Northesk (1758-1831). Admiral. He served with Nelson at Trafalgar in 1805.

COLLINGWOOD, Cuthbert, 1st Baron Collingwood (1750-1810). Vice-admiral. He was a lieutenant on Nelson's ship, 1778, and later commanded his own ship in the Mediterranean. Made a Vice-admiral in 1804, he took over command on Nelson's death at Trafalgar, 1805. Died at sea.

CRUIKSHANK, George (1792-1878). Illustrator and caricaturist. He began drawing at an early age, his first recorded illustration being the frontispiece to *The Beggar's Carnival*. He executed many etchings and engravings on wood, and was the illustrator of Dickens's *Oliver Twist* and *Sketches by Boz* and of Ainsworth's *Jack Sheppard*. (Cruikshank in fact claimed that he suggested the story and many of the incidents in *Oliver Twist*.) Collections of his works are in the Victoria and Albert Museum and the British Museum. (Disinterred from Kensal Green and buried here)

DANCE, George, the Elder (1700-68). He was an architect and surveyor to London Corporation. He designed the Mansion House in London in 1739.

DANCE, George, the Younger (1741-1825). Architect of many churches and other buildings. He rebuilt Newgate Prison, 1770.

FLEMING, Sir Alexander (1881-1955). Bacteriologist. Born in Lochfield, Ayrshire. Professor at London University. He discovered lysozyme, 1929, and in

1945 shared the Nobel Prize for Medicine for the discovery of penicillin in 1928. (Ashes deposited in crypt)

FOLEY, John Henry, R.A. (1818-74). Irish sculptor, who trained at the Academy Schools, London. His statues can be seen in Westminster Abbey, Mansion House— etc. He designed the seal of the Confederate States of America.

FREYBERG, Bernard Cyril, 1st Baron, V.C., D.S.O. (1889-1963). A remarkable soldier serving in Gallipoli and France. He was awarded the D.S.O. early in his career, when, swimming ashore from a destroyer in the Gulf of Xeros, on the eve of landing troops, he lit flares on the peninsula to deceive enemy tanks as to the landing point. He was wounded nine times in the last year of the First World War. Commanded New Zealand Expeditionary Forces in the Second World War. Governor-General of New Zealand, 1946-52.

FUSELI, Henry (1741-1825). Painter. He was born, Johann Heinrich Fuessli in Zurich, the son of an artist. He came to England in 1763 and was encouraged to paint by Sir Joshua Reynolds. He drew inspiration from Shakespeare, Dante and Milton. His painting outraged some of his contemporaries because of his aggressive sexual approach.

HAMILTON, General Sir Ian Standish Monteith, G.C.B., G.C.M.G., D.S.O. (1853-1947). He saw action in the Afghan War of 1878-79 and the Boer War. He commanded the force that landed on the Gallipoli peninsula in 1915, and was later the subject of an inquiry into the failure of this mission. Author of *Gallipoli Diary*.

HUNT, William Holman, O.M. (1827-1910). Pre-Raphaelite painter. Son of a warehouseman, he entered the Royal Academy in 1844. He started a life-long friendship with Millais, and the two of them, with Rossetti, formed the Pre-Raphaelite brotherhood in 1848. Among

his best-known paintings are *The Scapegoat* and *The Light of the World*.

JACKSON, Major Frederick (1860-1938). Soldier and polar explorer. He discovered and mapped the greater part of Franz Josef Land.

JELLICO, John Rushworth, 1st Earl (1859-1935) British naval officer who commanded the British fleet at the Battle of Jutland, 1916.

LANDSEER, Sir Edwin Henry (1802-73). Animal painter. He studied under his father John Landseer, and exhibited at the Royal Academy at the age of thirteen. He was elected R.A. in 1831, and knighted in 1850. Probably the most popular artist of his time. He completed the lions in Trafalgar Square, 1866.

LAWRENCE, Sir Thomas (1769-1830). Painter, and president of the Royal Academy. He is noted for his portraits— e.g., Mrs Siddons, J.P. Kemble as Hamlet—, etc.—many of which can be seen in London, including some at the National Gallery. He was buried with many honours in the Cathedral.

LEIGHTON, Frederick, Baron Leighton of Stretton (1830-96). Painter. He studied art at Frankfurt and Rome. Elected President of the Royal Academy in 1878. A prolific painter, most of his work is classical in subject. His Kensington house is now public property.

MILLAIS, Sir John Everett (1829-96). Pre-Raphaelite painter and illustrator. He studied at the Royal Academy and first exhibited there in 1846. He painted many well-known pictures, one of which, *Christ in the House of his Parents*, 1850, caused a storm of protest. Elected R.A. in 1863.

MUNNINGS, Sir Alfred James (1878-1959). Painter. He lived and painted in East Anglia and his main subjects were hunting scenes and the Suffolk country-side. Elected R.A. in 1925 and President 1944-9. (His ashes are buried in the crypt)

MYLNE, Robert, F.R.S. (1733-1810). Architect, Designer of Blackfriars Bridge and engineer of the New River Company. He was also superintendent in charge of the maintenance of St Paul's Cathedral.

NELSON, Horatio, Viscount Nelson (1758-1805). Vice-admiral. Nelson joined the navy in 1770 and suffered ill-health during his early career. He was unemployed for six years, but was put in command of seamen and marines at Bastia. In 1794 he lost the sight of his right eye at Calvi, in Corsica. He was promoted to Rear-admiral for harassing the French and preventing their coastal trade. Ill-health struck again and he had to return home, where he was created a Viscount in 1801. On his recovery he was appointed to the Mediterranean, and in 1805 fought the Battle of Trafalgar. During this battle Nelson was shot down by a musket fired from the mizzentop of the *Redoutable,* which Nelson's ship, the *Victory,* had engaged. He died three hours later, and was given a public funeral at St Paul's. The casket containing his body was made by Benedetto da Rovezzano and was originally intended for the body of Cardinal Wolsey.

Horatio Nelson

NELSON, William, 1st Earl Nelson (1757-1835). Brother of Horatio Nelson. He was Rector of Brandon Parva in South Norfolk, and is interesting mainly for his correspondence with his brother.

OPIE, John (1761-1807). Painter, known as the 'Cornish Wonder'. He was elected R.A. in 1788 and Professor of Painting in 1805. He painted portraits and historical subjects. His portraits include Dr Johnson and Southey, the poet.

PARRY, Sir Charles Hubert Hastings (1848-1918). Director of the Royal College of Music. Composer of music for solo voices, chorus and orchestra, and author of Volume iii, the *Oxford History of Music,* etc.

POYNTER, Sir Edward John (1836-1919). Painter. He studied in Paris under Gleyre. He became the first Slade Professor of Fine Art and was elected R.A. in 1876. Director of the National Gallery, 1894-1904. His best-known painting is the *Meeting of Solomon and the Queen of Sheba.*

REID DICK, Sir William (1879-1961). Scottish sculptor. He was well-known for his figure studies. He worked on the Kitchener Memorial Chapel in St Paul's, the RAF memorial in London, and sculpted the lion for the Menin Gate at Ypres. Elected R.A. in 1928. (Ashes buried here)

RENNIE, John (1761-1821). Civil engineer, born in Scotland. He had a great reputation as a designer of canals, locks and bridges. He constructed Waterloo Bridge (1810-17) and Southwark Bridge (1815-19) and designed London Bridge which, however, was not completed until 1831.

REYNOLDS, Sir Joshua (1723-92). Considered by many to be the greatest portrait painter that England has produced. Born in Devon. Foundation President of the Royal Academy. He was acquainted with

Garrick, Goldsmith and Samuel Johnson, and suggested the founding of the Literary Club in 1764.

ROBERTS, Frederick Sleigh, 1st Earl of Kandahar, Pretoria and Waterford (1832-1914). Field-marshal, known as 'Bobs'. As a Staff Officer during the Indian Mutiny, he fought in many actions and won the V.C. for an action at Khudaganj where he saved the life of an Indian. He was at the relief of Lucknow and relieved Kandahar, 1880. He became Commander-in-Chief in India and was made Commander-in-Chief of the army in South Africa where his great ability altered the course of the war. Author of *Forty-One Years in India*.

SMART, Christopher (1722-71). Poet. Educated at Cambridge where he was made a Fellow and was a contemporary of Thomas Gray, the poet. He contributed amusing verses to a magazine under the name of 'Ebenezer Pentweazle'. His translation of Horace brought riches to the booksellers but little to him. Later he was committed to a lunatic asylum where he is said to have composed his *A Song to David*, part of which he wrote on the walls of his cell. (In churchyard)

SULLIVAN, Sir Arthur Seymour (1842-1900). Composer. He studied at the Royal Academy of Music and at Leipzig, and was an organist and choirmaster. He became first Principal of the National Training School of Music. In collaboration with W.S. Gilbert he produced a series of comic operas, for which he composed the music, and the famous partnership was formed. He also wrote the music for *Onward Christian Soldiers, The Lost Chord*, etc.

TURNER, Joseph Mallord William (1775-1851). Landscape painter and water-colourist. Son of a London barber. Even at a very early age he was able to sell his drawings. He was admitted to Reynolds's studio, and had his first painting accepted by the Royal Academy at the age of fifteen. His early work shows the influence of the Old Masters, but about 1835 he began to develop his own style. His most famous painting is *The Fighting Téméraire* (1839); his Venice pictures were produced in 1843. Towards the end of his life Turner became soured with the world and threatened to make his shroud out of his own painting, *The Building of Carthage*. He requested that he should be buried as near as possible to his old master, Joshua Reynolds.

WELLESLEY, Arthur, 1st Duke of Wellington (1769-1852). Field-marshal, known as the 'Iron Duke'. Educated at Eton and Angers Military Academy. His army career was distinguished, despite some setbacks against the French. In 1815 he was in command of the British forces at the Battle of Waterloo, where he repulsed all French attacks until joined by the Prussians together with whom he advanced on Paris. In 1817 he was given Apsley House and Strathfieldsaye by the nation. He was Prime Minister, 1828-30, and put through the Catholic Emancipation Act. The national monument to Wellington stands on the north aisle of the nave and was designed by Alfred Stevens.

WEST, Benjamin (1738-1820). Painter of historical subjects. He was born in America, of Quaker parents, and was self-taught. He was an original member of the Royal Academy and showed his work at the first exhibition there in 1769. He became President of the Royal Academy in 1792.

WILSON, Sir Henry Hughes (1864-1922). Field-marshal who served in the First World War. He was largely responsible for the readiness of the army to meet the enemy in 1914. He was later made M.P. for North Down, 1922. His views on the

Irish Question made him many enemies, and on 22nd June 1922 he was assassinated by two members of Sinn Fein.

WREN, Sir Christopher (1632-1723). Architect, scientist and mathematician. Acknowledged as the greatest British architect. He was almost entirely self-taught as an architect and, though imperfectly trained, improved his technique by a great deal of practical experience. When one considers his works it is difficult to understand how one man could accomplish so much in a lifetime. Architecture was only one aspect of his many-sided genius, he was also greatly respected for his knowledge as a scientist and mathematician. Born at East Knoyle, Wiltshire, he was a brilliant scholar at Oxford where he later became Professor of Astronomy. Had his plans for London, after the Great Fire of 1666, been put into effect, London would have become the most beautiful city in Europe. He designed and rebuilt St Paul's 1675-1716, and built fifty-two other churches in London. His only weakness was his poor business ability and in this field he was often abused.

Wren's Tomb

SKETCH PLAN OF ST PAUL'S CATHEDRAL CRYPT

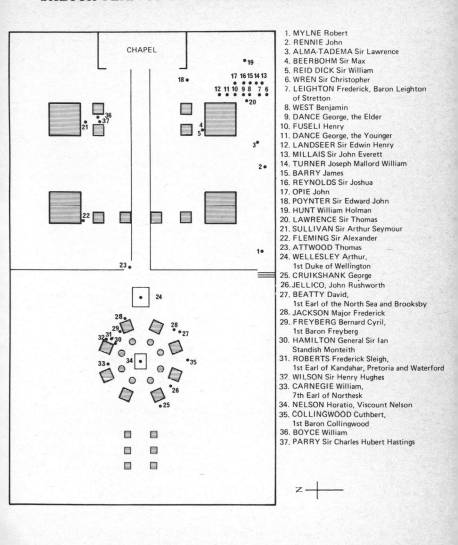

CHAPEL

1. MYLNE Robert
2. RENNIE John
3. ALMA-TADEMA Sir Lawrence
4. BEERBOHM Sir Max
5. REID DICK Sir William
6. WREN Sir Christopher
7. LEIGHTON Frederick, Baron Leighton
   of Stretton
8. WEST Benjamin
9. DANCE George, the Elder
10. FUSELI Henry
11. DANCE George, the Younger
12. LANDSEER Sir Edwin Henry
13. MILLAIS Sir John Everett
14. TURNER Joseph Mallord William
15. BARRY James
16. REYNOLDS Sir Joshua
17. OPIE John
18. POYNTER Sir Edward John
19. HUNT William Holman
20. LAWRENCE Sir Thomas
21. SULLIVAN Sir Arthur Seymour
22. FLEMING Sir Alexander
23. ATTWOOD Thomas
24. WELLESLEY Arthur,
    1st Duke of Wellington
25. CRUIKSHANK George
26. JELLICO, John Rushworth
27. BEATTY David,
    1st Earl of the North Sea and Brooksby
28. JACKSON Major Frederick
29. FREYBERG Bernard Cyril,
    1st Baron Freyberg
30. HAMILTON General Sir Ian
    Standish Monteith
31. ROBERTS Frederick Sleigh,
    1st Earl of Kandahar, Pretoria and Waterford
32. WILSON Sir Henry Hughes
33. CARNEGIE William,
    7th Earl of Northesk
34. NELSON Horatio, Viscount Nelson
35. COLLINGWOOD Cuthbert,
    1st Baron Collingwood
36. BOYCE William
37. PARRY Sir Charles Hubert Hastings

Holborn
CHURCH OF THE HOLY SEPULCHRE OR ST SEPULCHRE
(Giltspur Street)

Underground: St Paul's   Buses: 8, 22, 25

The largest parish church in the City. It was originally dedicated to St Edmund, King of East Anglia, but was renamed at the time of the Crusades. In the eighteenth century the graveyard was continually robbed of its corpses by body-snatchers who sold them to lecturers at St Bartholomew's Hospital. An underground passage once led from the church to Newgate Prison, and a bell kept in the church was rung on the morning of executions.

ASCHAM, Roger (1515-68). Tutor to Queen Elizabeth I and Lady Jane Grey. A very skilled archer, he was the author of a book called *Toxophilus,* 1545, for which he was awarded a pension for life by Henry VIII.

HOLGATE or HOLDEGATE, Robert (*c.* 1481-1555). Archbishop of York. Chaplain to Henry VIII. He was deprived of his See and imprisoned for being married in 1554. The founder of grammar schools at York and elsewhere.

SMITH, Captain John (1580-1631). Soldier and colonist. After travelling in south-eastern Europe he set out with the Virginia colonists in 1606, and later became head of the colony. He is said to have been rescued by the Princess Pocahontas in 1607 after being taken prisoner by the Indians.

WOOD, Sir Henry Joseph (1869-1944). (Musicians' chapel). Famous conductor and musician. It was in this church that the young Henry Wood learned to play the organ. He conducted the first promenade concerts, now known as the Henry Wood Promenade Concerts, and also composed songs and cantatas. (Ashes buried under the central window)

Coleman Street   # ST STEPHEN'S CHURCH

Underground: Bank or Moorgate   Buses: 8, 22, 25

Churches have stood on this site from the twelfth century, the last one being a Wren church built in 1676. The churchyard was one of the chief plague burial grounds in the city. The church was destroyed during the Second World War and a Swiss bank built on the site.

KEATS, Thomas (d. 1804). He was the father of John Keats, the poet, and worked as head ostler in a livery-stable.

KEATS, Tom (1799-1818). He was the brother of John Keats, and died of consumption. His brother nursed him in his last illness, and was thus later able to recognize the symptoms of the same illness in himself.

Walbrook   # ST STEPHEN'S CHURCH

Underground: Bank   Buses: 6, 8, 11, 15, 22, 25

The first church was probably built on the west bank of the Walbrook. The second church was built on the site of the present building (on the east bank). It is thought to be Wren's masterpiece, after St Paul's, and was completed in 1679.

HODGES, Dr Nathaniel (1629-88). Physician. He treated patients throughout the plague in 1665 and published his own account in 1672. He is thought to be the original Dr Heath in Defoe's *Diary of the Plague Year* and the doctor in Harrison Ainsworth's *Old St Paul's*.

VANBRUGH or VANBURGH, Sir John (1664-1726). Architect, playwright and herald; designer of Blenheim Palace and Castle Howard. Clarenceux King-at-Arms, 1704-26. Disraeli said of him, 'an imaginative artist, whose critics I wish no bitterer fate, than not to live in his splendid creations'. A Dr Evans wrote his epitaph: 'Lie heavy on him, earth, for he/Laid many a heavy load on thee'.

Fleet Street

Underground: Temple

THE TEMPLE CHURCH

Buses: 6, 11, 15

Founded in the twelfth century but very much restored. It was later bombed in the Second World War and rebuilt keeping to the original, circular ground-floor plan. The Knights Templars were formed in Jerusalem in 1119-20 after the First Crusade.

BARRINGTON, Daines (1727-1800). Lawyer, antiquary and naturalist. He is said to have encouraged Gilbert White of Selborne to write his *Natural History of Selborne*.

COKE, Sir Edward (1552-1634). Judge and writer on law. He was one of the most outspoken men of his day and provoked James I by speaking against the Spanish Marriage and denouncing his interference with the liberties of Parliament. He was imprisoned in the Tower in 1622, later released and became an M.P. for·Buckinghamshire in 1628.

GOLDSMITH, Oliver (1728-74). Author. He was educated in Ireland and studied medicine in Edinburgh. After travelling extensively abroad, where he visited Voltaire, he came to London, destitute, in 1776. There he met Dr Johnson and joined his Club. Johnson praised his poem *The Traveller*, 1764, and sold his *Vicar of Wakefield*. Besides many novels, Goldsmith also wrote poetry and plays— e.g., *The Deserted Village* and *She Stoops to Conquer*.

HARE, Sir Nicholas (d. 1557). Judge. M.P. for Lancaster, and Speaker of the House of Commons in 1540. He defended Wolsey in 1530.

HOWELL, James (*c.* 1594-1666). Author and traveller. He went on many diplomatic missions to Spain and the Middle East. In 1643-51 he was a Royalist prisoner in the Fleet Prison. He was a friend of Ben Jonson.

MARTIN, Richard (1570-1618). Recorder of London. He was expelled from the Middle Temple for a brawl with his friend, Sir John Davies. Ben Jonson dedicated his *Poetaster* to him.

PLOWDEN, Edmund (1518-85). Jurist and barrister at the Middle Temple. He was M.P. for Wallingford, 1553, and Reading, 1554, but, as he was a Catholic, public life was closed to him on Elizabeth's succession. He found great fame as a jurist and is immortalized in the saying, 'The case is altered, quoth Plowden'.

THURLOW, Edward, 1st Baron Thurlow (1731-1806). Lord Chancellor. He was educated at Cambridge, but was sent down for misconduct and became a barrister. In 1770 he was appointed Solicitor-general, and in 1771 Attorney-general. He presided at Warren Hastings's trial in 1788, and also defended the interests of slave-traders. He once fought a duel with the Duke of Hamilton's agent.

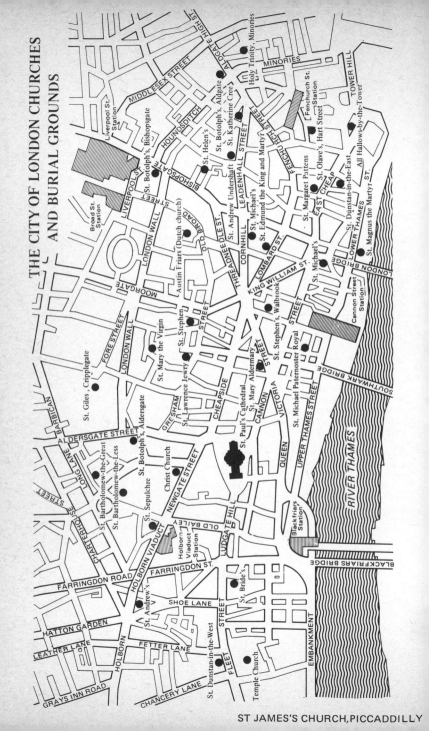

THE CITY OF LONDON CHURCHES AND BURIAL GROUNDS

ST JAMES'S CHURCH, PICCADDILLY

CITY OF WESTMINSTER

Victoria Street   CHRIST CHURCH *(Broadway)*

Underground: Victoria St James's Park   Buses: 11, 24, 29

The church was built in 1843 on the site of the New Chapel, which dated from 1636.
There was a burial ground here as far back as 1627, which was mentioned by Pepys in
1665. In 1954 the church was pulled down.

BLOOD, Thomas, Colonel (*c.* 1618-80). Adventurer. He owned estates in Ireland, but they were forfeited at the Restoration. Among his exploits were an attempt to assassinate the Duke of Ormonde, and a plan to steal the crown jewels. He actually made off with the crown and orb, but was arrested. He later managed to win Charles II's favour, and regained his Irish estates.

HOLLAR, Wenceslaus (1607-77). Engraver. Originally a native of Prague, he then lived in Germany and Belgium, and was brought to England by Thomas Howard, second Earl of Arundel. He was teacher of drawing to Prince Charles (later Charles II) and also designed a very fine map of London after the Great Fire of 1666.

WALLER, Sir William (*c.* 1597-1668). Parliamentary General, nicknamed 'William the Conqueror'. He took several Royalist towns during the Civil War, and also defeated the Royalists in Wales. He was later arrested by Cromwell for actively plotting a Royalist uprising. He was once fined for brawling at court.

South Audley Street
     GROSVENOR CHAPEL *(Between Mount Street and South Street)*

Underground: Bond Street   Buses: 6, 8, 12, 15 –etc. *to Oxford Stree*

This chapel was built in the eighteenth century as part of the Grosvenor Square scheme,
and is one of the few chapels in this scheme to have survived.

CARTER, Elizabeth (1717-1806). Writer. She wrote for the *Gentleman's Magazine*, published poems and studied classical and modern languages. A friend of Dr Johnson.

MALET (originally Malloch), David (*c.* 1705-65). Poet and writer. Author of *William and Margaret*, a famous ballad of the time, and possibly author of *Rule Britannia*. He also produced plays at Drury Lane.

MONTAGU, Lady Mary Wortley (1689-1762). After her visit to Constantinople with her husband, who was Ambassador there, she introduced the practice of inoculation for smallpox. She was also the author of several books. She quarrelled with Pope and was satirized by him.

PHILIPS, Ambrose (*c.* 1675-1744). Poet. His pastoral verse aroused the jealousy of Pope, who attacked Philips in his satires.

WHITEHEAD, William (1715-85). Poet Laureate, 1757. He produced plays at Drury Lane, and became Garrick's reader for the plays in which he performed.

WILKES, John (1727-97). Politician. After being educated at Leyden University he returned to London and became a prominent member of a group of pro-fligates known as the 'Medmenham Monks'. He was twice expelled from the House of Commons, and disgraced, for printing and publishing libellous matter in *The North Briton* and an article in the *St James's Chronicle*. Hogarth caricatured him.

ST ANNE'S CHURCH *(Wardour Street)*

The church was built in 1686, possibly by Wren, but the tower was added later and is the only part of the building that remains. Theodore, King of Corsica, and Hazlitt are buried in the churchyard.

HAZLITT, William (1778-1830). Essayist and the author of several biographies including the *Life of Napoleon Buonaparte.* He was a contributor to the *Examiner* and the *Edinburgh Review.* He also studied painting and gave lectures on modern philosophy, and was a famous critic, particularly of Shakespeare.

PITT, Thomas, 2nd Baron Camelford (1775-1804). He led a very stormy life in the Navy, where his adventures included being put ashore at Hawaii for insubordination and having to work his passage home, and shooting a lieutenant during a dispute. His life in London was no less notorious, and he was finally shot dead in a duel near Holland House by a Captain Best.

TAYLOR, Brook (1685-1731). Mathematician. He wrote works on perspective and became very interested in the planetary laws of motion. He published *Linear Perspective* in 1715.

THEODORE ETIENNE of Corsica (d. 1756). The king of Corsica who lost his throne in 1736. Something of an adventurer, he came to England in exile and was imprisoned for debt in the Fleet Prison.

WILLIAMS, David (1738-1816). Founder of the Royal Literary Fund. He was a dissenting ordained minister who also opened schools in London.

Strand ST CLEMENT DANES

This church was built in 1681 by Wren on the site of an earlier church which was believed to be the burial place of the Dane, Harold Harefoot (d. 1040). The present church was gutted in 1941, but was rebuilt and is now the church of the Royal Air Force. There were burials in the churchyard until 1853. Burials in the crypt were prohibited in 1851, but in 1941 the crypt was explored for the first time in a hundred years and was found still to have a layer of earth with some human remains. Among those buried here are John Donne's wife and William Mountford, the actor, who was murdered.

BERKELEY, Bishop George (1685-1753). Bishop of Cloyne. He studied philosophy and was acquainted with Addison, Swift and Pope.

BYER, Nicholas (d. 1681). Painter. He had a considerable reputation for his portraits, the subjects of which were usually historical or Norwegian. He was said to be the first person buried in the church itself.

DONNE, Anne (d. 1617). Wife of John Donne, Dean of St Paul's, who preached a sermon at her funeral.

GRANVILLE or GRENVILLE, George, Viscount Lansdowne (1667-1735). Privy Councillor, also poet and dramatist. He appeared in his own plays at Lincoln's Inn Fields and Drury Lane. His poems were praised by Pope. He was imprisoned in the Tower, 1715-17, as a suspected Jacobite.

KITCHINER, Dr William (c. 1775-1827). Author of *Apicius Redivivus* or 'The Cooks Oracle' and works on science and music.

LEE, Nathaniel (c. 1653-92). Author of many plays, mainly tragedies from classical history. He was described as a 'good for nothing dramatist'.

LOWEN, John (d. 1653). One of the original actors who appeared in Shakespeare's plays.

MOUNTFORD, William (c. 1664-92). An actor who was murdered in Howard Street by Lord Mohun and his associates. He was a friend of Judge Jeffreys.

OTWAY, Thomas (1652-85). Dramatist. He tried his hand at acting but was unsuccessful. His works were translated into French, German, Dutch and Russian. His best-known work is *Venice Preserved*, 1682.

PIERCE, Edward (d. 1698). Sculptor. Worked under Wren on City churches, also employed at Hampton Court and Whitehall.

RYMER, Thomas (1641-1713). Author, archaeologist and compiler of *Foedera*. He became a barrister at Gray's Inn in 1673.

SALE, George (c. 1697-1736). Translator of the Koran. His is the best version in any language. His oriental manuscripts are in the Bodleian Library.

SPILLER, James (1692-1730). Comedian and original Mat o' the Mint in *The Beggar's Opera*. He was frequently imprisoned in the Marshalsea for nonpayment of debts. A pub which he frequented near Clare Market was named Spiller's Head after him.

Piccadilly

Underground: Piccadilly

ST JAMES'S CHURCH

Buses: 9, 14, 22, 25, 38

This has been regarded as the most fashionable church in London. It was built by Wren in 1680, with funds supplied by Henry Jermyn, Earl of St Albans (patron of Cowley and reputed husband of Henrietta Maria, widow of Charles I). There are graves in both church and churchyard, and they include that of James Gillray and the fourth Duke of Queensberry.

AKENSIDE, Mark, F.R.S. (1721-70). Physician and poet. He was at one time Doctor to Cambridge University, and Physician to the Queen in 1761. His collected poems were published in 1772, and he was also a frequent contributor to the *Gentleman's Magazine*.

ARBUTHNOT, Dr John (1667-1735). Physician to Queen Anne in 1709. Besides publishing medical and scientific works, he also wrote the *History of John Bull* and many witty and poetical works. A friend of Pope, Swift and Gay.

BROOKES, Joshua, F.R.S. (1761-1833). Anatomist who taught in London and formed a large private museum.

COTTON, Charles (1630-87). A poet of Beresford, Staffordshire. As well as poetry he published several translations, notably of Montaigne's *Essays* in 1685. He was a friend of Izaak Walton, and published a 'second part' of Walton's *Compleat Angler* in 1676.

DAHL, Michael (1656-1743). Portrait painter, born in Stockholm. He became very popular and was patronized by Queen Anne.

DELANEY, Mary, *née* Granville (1700-88). Inventor of the 'flower mosaic' in 1774 and a friend of Swift and Fanny Burney.

DODSLEY, James (1724-97). Bookseller and brother of the poet and editor, Robert Dodsley.

DOUGLAS, William, 3rd Earl of March and 4th Duke of Queensberry (1724-1810). Known as 'Old Q', he was notorious for his riotous and dissolute life. He tried to develop horse-racing into a science. He was a friend of the Prince of Wales, and was removed from the office of Lord of the Bedchamber in 1789 for having recommended a regency. (Buried under the altar)

D'URFEY, Tom (1653-1723). Dramatist and poet. He was buried at the expense of the Earl of Dorset.

GILLRAY, James (1757-1815). Caricaturist. Many of his caricatures ridiculed the French Revolution and the habits of the royal family. He also did two serious portraits, of Pitt and of himself, which are in the National Portrait Gallery. He became an imbecile in 1811.

HARLOW, George Henry (1787-1819). Painter, and a declared opponent of the Royal Academy. His group scenes include the Kembles and Sarah Siddons. He was invited to paint a self-portrait for the Uffizi Gallery in Florence.

HUNTER, Dr William (1718-83). Surgeon and Physician to Queen Charlotte in 1764. He was the first Professor of Anatomy at the Royal Academy in 1768.

HUYSMANS, Jacob (c. 1636-96). A painter who came to England in 1660. His portraits include Catherine of Braganza and Izaak Walton.

SIDNEY, Henry, Earl of Romney (1641-1704). Partisan of William of Orange. In 1679 he was sent as envoy to The Hague where he gained William's confidence and gave him a secret invitation to come to England. Later he accompanied William to England and Ireland. He was Lord Lieutenant of Ireland in 1692.

STILLINGFLEET, Benjamin (1702-71). Botanist and author. He introduced the Linnean system into England, and first proposed the English names for types of grass. He also wrote librettos for oratorios. The term 'blue-stocking' originates from Stillingfleet's fashion of dress.

VAN DER VELDE, Willem, the Elder (d. 1693). Marine painter. Born in Leyden, where he was originally a sailor-boy, he came to England in 1675.

Parliament Square   ST MARGARET'S CHURCH

Underground: Westminster

Buses: 3, 11, 12, 24–etc.

The present church dates back to 1504, but there was an earlier church on this site. The churchyard has been the scene of several macabre events. Several of Cromwell's friends and family, including his mother and Thomas May, the historian, were removed from Westminster Abbey and flung into a pit in St Margaret's churchyard at the time of the Restoration. Among those buried here are William Caxton and Sir Walter Raleigh.

BRANCH, William (d. 1555). He had his right hand cut off and was later burned alive in the churchyard for attacking a priest John Chelton, as he was saying mass.

CAXTON, William (c. 1422-91). First and most famous of all English printers. In 1441 he went to Bruges where he started a business, returning to England in 1476. He found favour with Edward IV, Richard III and Henry VII, and established a press at Westminster, 1477-91.

CHURCHYARD, Thomas (c. 1520-1604). Writer who led a wandering life, partly as a soldier and partly as a hanger-on at Court. He published many verse and prose works.

CUTLER, Sir John (c. 1608-93). London merchant and Treasurer of St Paul's. He founded a lectureship on mechanics at Gresham College and was benefactor of the College of Musicians in the parish of St Margaret's. Personally very miserly, he occasioned Wycherley's *Praise of Avarice,* and was the miser mentioned by Pope (in *Moral Essays,* iii).

ELSYNGE, Henry (1598-1654). Clerk of the House of Commons. He resigned his post to avoid involvement in the proceedings against Charles I in 1648.

FERRABOSCO, Alphonso (d. 1661). Composer and Musician in Ordinary, 1628, and 'viol' in the King's band.

GADBURY, John (1627-1704). Astrologer and maker of almanacs. He published accounts of three comets in 1665. In 1690 he was wrongly accused of plotting against William III.

HARRINGTON, James (1611-77). Political theorist and author of several works. Groom of the Bedchamber to Charles I at Holmby and the Isle of Wight. He published *The Commonwealth of Oceana* in 1656.

HICKES, Dr George (1642-1715). Vicar of All Hallows, Barking in 1680. He was expelled from his living for refusing to take the oath of allegiance to William and Mary in 1690.

RALEIGH, Carew (1606-66). Politician. He was the son of Sir Walter Raleigh and Governor of Jersey, 1660.

RALEIGH or RALEGH, Sir Walter (c. 1552-1618). Military and naval commander, author, discoverer of Virginia, and favourite of Queen Elizabeth I. He is credited with the introduction of tobacco and the potato into England. He was committed to the Tower for a while by Elizabeth because of an affair with Elizabeth Throgmorton, whom he later married. In 1603 he was committed to the Tower again on a charge of conspiracy against James I, and found guilty. He was later reprieved, although kept imprisoned until 1616, when he was allowed to undertake another (unsuccessful) expedition in search of gold. During this expedition a Spanish settlement was burned on the orders of his second-in-command, Raleigh being ill at the time. This was strictly contrary to the policy of the English Parliament, and Raleigh was executed on his return to England.

SKELTON, John (c. 1460-1529). Poet and one-time tutor to Prince Henry, later Henry VIII. He was admitted to orders in 1498 and was patronized by Wolsey, whom he attacked in his poems, however, and by whom he is said to have been imprisoned. He was created poet laureate by the Universities of Oxford and Cambridge, and possibly by the Crown.

UDALL or UVEDALE, Nicholas (1505-56). Dramatist and scholar. Headmaster of Eton and later of Winchester, and also Vicar of Braintree, Essex, and Rector of Calborne, in the Isle of Wight. Playwright to Queen Mary. Among his works are a translation of part of Erasmus's *Apophthegms,* and *Ralph Roister Doister* — the earliest known English comedy.

There was a church here as early as the thirteenth century. A later church was built by Henry VIII who was said to have objected to corpses being carried past St James's Palace for burial at St Margaret's, Westminster. The churchyard formerly covered much ground around the church. To the north-east was a monks' burial ground, while to the south was the burial place of the Thames watermen. The National Gallery now stands on the site of the main burial ground, and when workmen were preparing the ground they found the bodies of George Heriot, the banker, and Jack Sheppard, the highwayman, lying next to each other. Buried in this churchyard are Francis Bacon and Thomas Chippendale.

BACON, Francis, 1st Baron Verulam (1561-1626). Lord Chancellor and famous author of philosophical and literary works. He was chief prosecutor at the trial of Somerset in 1616 and also attended Raleigh's trial. He was later charged before the House of Lords with bribery and imprisoned in the Tower for a short while. It was his ambition to create a new system of philosophy. His *Essays* form one of his most important works.

BANNISTER, Charles (c. 1738-1804). Actor and singer. His first London performance was at the Haymarket Theatre, and he later appeared at Covent Garden and Drury Lane. (Buried in a vault under the communion table)

BOYLE, Robert (1627-91). Philosopher and chemist who established the proportional relation between elasticity and pressure, known as 'Boyle's Law'. Author of *New Experiments Physico-Mechanical*, 1660.

CHIPPENDALE, Thomas (d. 1779). Furniture maker who lived and worked near the church and who gave his name to the style of solid, ornate and graceful furniture he produced.

CHURCHILL, Sir Winston (c. 1620-88). Historian and politician who became impoverished by the civil war. He was the father of John Churchill, the first Duke of Marlborough.

COVENTRY, Henry (1619-86). Secretary of State. He attended Charles II in exile. (Tomb in present church)

DAVIES, Sir John (1569-1626). He was Attorney-general for Ireland and also a poet.

DOBSON, William Charles Thomas (1817-98). English portrait painter, known as the 'English Van Dyck'. He exhibited at the Royal Academy from 1842. (On the site of the National Gallery)

FARQUHAR, George (1678-1707). Dramatist. He was originally an actor, but turned to writing plays after accidentally wounding a fellow actor. (On the site of the National Gallery)

GODFREY, Sir Edmund Berry (1621-78). Justice of the Peace for Westminster, he was a zealous Protestant who, nevertheless, lived on excellent terms with the Catholics. However, Godfrey was found dead in a ditch on Primrose Hill, transfixed by his own sword, but with marks of strangulation, and three of the Queen's servants (one Protestant and two Catholic) were hanged for this crime, despite their declarations of innocence. The evidence given by Miles Prance, a Catholic silversmith, was given under torture and later repudiated. The crime was perhaps instigated by Titus Oates.

GWYN, Nell (1650-1687). Actress and favourite mistress of Charles II. Her first name was really Eleanor and she started her career selling oranges in the Theatre Royal, Drury Lane, making her first stage appearance as 'Cydaria' in Dryden's *Indian Emperor*. She was illiterate, but comedy came 'natural' to her. One of her sons by Charles was made Duke of St Albans.

HERIOT, George (1563-1624). Banker and founder of Heriot's Hospital, Edinburgh. He was Jeweller to James I and VI. Scott is said to have based his character 'Jingling Geordie' from *The Fortunes of Nigel* on him.

HILLIARD, Nicholas (1537-1619). The first, and probably the greatest English miniature painter. He painted a miniature of himself at thirteen years of age, and a portrait of Mary, Queen of Scots.

LACY, John (d. 1681). Actor, dramatist, dancing master and soldier, attached to Charles II's company of actors. (On the site of the National Gallery)

LAGUERRE, Louis (1663-1721). Painter, of Spanish origin. He studied drawing at the school of the French Academy and painted the ceilings and halls at Burleigh House, Blenheim, etc.

LANIER, Nicholas (1568-1646). Etcher.

MAYERNE, Sir Theodore Turquet (1573-1655). Physician to James I and Charles I. He was the author of a text on precautions against the plague and an account of typhoid fever. (Tomb now in new church)

MOHUN, Charles, 5th Baron (*c.* 1675-1712). Duellist. He was killed in a duel with the Duke of Hamilton, in which the Duke was also mortally wounded. Thackeray used this incident in *Henry Esmond*.

ROUBILIAC or ROUBILLAC, Louis François (1695-1762). Sculptor, born in Lyons, France. His work includes monuments and busts of well-known people of his day, many of which can be seen in Westminster Abbey—e.g., the Nightingale monument. (In present church)

SHEPPARD, Jack (1702-24). Highwayman who escaped from prison several times before he was finally put to death. He was hanged and his body buried in the part of the churchyard now covered by the National Gallery. His remains were found there with those of Heriot, the banker, when the site was being prepared. The cell from which he escaped is on display in the Tussaud Waxworks at Baker Street.

STANLEY, Thomas (1625-78). Classical scholar, translator of the Greek and Latin poets, and author of a *History of Philosophy*.

STUART, James (1713-88). Painter and architect who introduced the Greek style of architecture into London. He was known as 'Athenian Stuart'.

TAYLOR, John (1580-1653). The 'water poet'. He was a Thames waterman who expressed himself in rollicking prose and verse. He arranged the water-pageant at the marriage of Princess Elizabeth in 1613. He tried to sail from London to Queenborough in a brown-paper boat and was almost drowned. (Old church)

TURNER, Anne (1576-1615). Hanged at Tyburn for helping the Countess of Essex in the poisoning of Sir Thomas Overbury. (On the site of the National Gallery)

VAN SOMER, Paul (1576-1621). The favourite portrait painter at the Court of James I. Born in Antwerp.

In the words of its designer, Inigo Jones, 'the handsomest barn in Europe'. It was rebuilt by Thomas Hardwick in 1798, after it had been destroyed by fire, and most of the gravestones were removed when the churchyard was levelled. Many of the famous are buried in vaults and precincts. It is known as the 'actors' church.

BURMAN, Thomas (1618-74). Sculptor. Chiefly remembered as the master of John Bushnell, the sculptor. (Buried in churchyard)

BUTLER, Samuel (1612-80). Satirist. Secretary to the Lord President of Wales, and Steward of Ludlow castle. He published *Hudibras,* 1663-8.

CARR or KER, Robert, Earl of Somerset (d. 1645). Originally private secretary to King James I. He was accused in 1615 of poisoning Overbury, to which his wife Frances, formerly Countess of Essex, pleaded guilty. He was held in the Tower until 1622, then pardoned.

DUVAL, Claude (1643-70). Highwayman born in France. He came to England at the Restoration and served under the Duke of Richmond. He took to robbing on the highways around London, and became well-known for his daring. He was said to have held up a lady's carriage and, although she had £400, he only robbed her of £100 on condition that she danced with him on the heath near Highgate. He was hanged at Tyburn, but was so popular a rogue that he was given a funeral at St Paul's, and it is thought they buried him under the central aisle of church with the epitaph—'Here lies Duval, reader if male thou art/ Look to thy purse, if female to thy heart'. There is some doubt as to whether his body is in the church now. (His burial record is in St Giles-in-the-Fields)

ESTCOURT, Richard (1688-1712). Actor and dramatist, who appeared at Drury Lane.

GIBBONS, Grinling (1648-1720). Wood carver, born at Rotterdam. He was engaged by Wren to carve stalls in St Paul's and many of his other London churches. His carvings are also in Canterbury Cathedral, Trinity College Cambridge, etc.

GIRTIN, Thomas (1775-1802). Water-colour painter. He was imprisoned for not completing his apprenticeship. Called 'the father of modern water-colour painting'. A friend of Turner.

GREAVES, Sir Edward (1608-80). Physician to Charles II. He studied at Padua and Leyden.

HAINES or HAYNES, Joseph (d. 1701). Known as 'Count Haines'. Dancer and actor at the Theatre Royal. He played Benito in Dryden's *Assignation,* a part written expressly for him. His finest part was Noll Bluff in Congreve's *Old Batchelor.*

HERBERT, Sir Henry (1595-1673). Master of the Revels. He was the brother of George Herbert, the poet. He claimed jurisdiction over all public entertainment and the right to license plays, poems, ballads and other entertainment.

HURST, Henry (1629-90). Nonconformist minister and outspoken antiCatholic preacher, who preached in the Covent Garden area.

KNELLER or KNILLER, John Zacharias (1644-1702). Painter of portraits, landscapes and architectural scenes. Brother of Sir Godfrey Kneller, the painter. He was born in Lübeck, but travelled with his brother and lived in England.

KYNASTON, Edward (c. 1640-1706). Actor. He appeared at the Cockpit Theatre Drury Lane in 1659. He played Cassio in *Othello* in 1682, and acted with Thomas Betterton. One of the last men to play female parts.

LELY, Sir Peter (1618-80). Portrait painter, born near Utrecht. He came to England in 1641 and was introduced to Charles I. He was favoured by both Cromwell and Charles II, painting the portraits of many of the beauties of the Court.

MACKLIN, Charles (c. 1697-1797). Actor and stage manager. Played at Drury Lane Theatre, 1733-48. Famous for his interpretation of Shylock. He wrote several plays—e.g., *The Man of the World*, 1781.

TEMPEST, Pierce (1653-1717). Print-maker, famous for his *Cryes of the City of London,* published 1711.

WISEMAN, Richard (c. 1622-76). Surgeon, imprisoned for assisting a Royalist in 1654. After the Restoration, in 1672, he became Master Surgeon to Charles II.

WYCHERLEY, William (c. 1640-1716). Dramatist. His first play, *Love in a Wood, or St James's Park,* was produced in 1671, and his last, *The Plain Dealer,* was performed at a theatre in Lincoln's Inn Fields. He was an intimate friend of Charles II's mistress, Barbara, Duchess of Cleveland, and a friend of Pope, who revised some of his writings. A member of the Inner Temple.

Strand

Underground: Charing Cross

SAVOY CHAPEL

Buses: 6, 9, 11, 15, 77

This chapel is also known as St Mary-le-Savoy, Chapel Royal of the Savoy. The church was built in 1505, by Henry VII, on the ruins of the old Palace of the Savoy. It was almost entirely rebuilt in 1721, and was made a Royal Chapel by George III. Badly damaged in 1864, it was repaired by Queen Victoria at her own expense. The chapel was notorious for the many clandestine marriages performed there.

CAMERON, Archibald (1707-53). Jacobite. He studied medicine in Scotland and became physician to the Stuart supporters. He was responsible for the escape of Prince Charles in 1746 and for this was arrested and executed at Tyburn. He was the last person to be executed for taking part in the 1745 Rebellion.

DE WINT, Peter (1784-1849). Landscape painter. A member of the Society of Painters in Water-colours, he also painted in oils. His subjects are mainly northern and eastern English landscapes.

DOUGLAS, Gawin or Gavin (c. 1474-1522). Scottish poet, Archbishop of St Andrews, 1514, and Bishop of Dunkeld,

1516-20. He translated the *Aeneid* with prologues, 1553, and was probably the first classical translator into the vernacular. He also wrote two allegorical poems, the best-known of which is *The Palice of Honour.* He died of the plague in 1522.

DURAS or DURFORT, Louis, Earl of Feversham (c. 1640-1709). A member of the French peerage who became a naturalized Englishman in 1665. He was later Lord Chamberlain to Queen Catherine and commander of James II's troops at the Battle of Sedgemoor, 1685.

HILTON, William, R.A. (1786-1839). Historical painter. He exhibited at the Royal Academy from 1803.

KILLIGREW, Henry (1613-1700). Master of the Savoy. He was chaplain to the King's army in 1642, and also published sermons and Latin verses.

WITHER or WITHERS, George (1588-1667). Poet, patronized by Princess Elizabeth. He was imprisoned in the Marshalsea for his abusive satire, but later became a Puritan. His reputation as a poet is based mainly on a collection of poems called *Juvenilia*, 1622.

Parliament Square

WESTMINSTER ABBEY

Underground: Westminster

Buses: 3, 11, 12, 24, 29, 53, 88, 159

The official title of Westminster Abbey is the Collegiate Church of Saint Peter in Westminster, a title which was bestowed upon it by Queen Elizabeth I. A church is believed to have been founded on this site as early as A.D. 616 by Mellitus, who was made Bishop of London by St Augustine. Later, in the eighth century, a Benedictine abbey called West Minster or Monastery was set up on the same site which was west of the city. The present building is a mixture of about six styles of architecture, although the main portion was built during the reign of Henry III.

It is regarded as Edward the Confessor's church as he designed it for his own burial. He was interred in front of the altar soon after its consecration. From then on coronations which took place near the tomb were considered to have greater sanctity, and many of Edward's eminent followers aspired to be buried near this place.

Throughout its history the Abbey has witnessed many moving funeral services, though a number of these took place at night, witnessed by a handful of people. On several occasions Abbey monuments have been damaged during violent scenes at funerals.

Of all the religious houses in Britain, the Abbey has been the last resting place of the greatest number of royal and illustrious people in British history.

NORTH TRANSEPT

CANNING, George (1770-1827). Statesman and a great orator who served under Pitt the Younger. He was made Prime Minister and Chancellor of the Exchequer by George IV in 1827. In 1808 he fought a duel with Castlereagh over the latter's policy at the War Office.

CAVENDISH, William, 1st Duke of Newcastle, K.G. (1592-1676), and his second Duchess, Margaret (c. 1624-1674). Distinguished patriot and statesman. He was a staunch Royalist and fought at Marston Moor, 1644. He lived in poverty in Holland until the Restoration when only part of his estate was restored. He was a patron of Ben Jonson and Dryden. His wife was a prolific writer—her effigy is seen holding an open book and pen case.

She had been a maid of honour to Henrietta Maria but after the Restoration was abused by Charles II's Court when she sought to recover her husband's estate.

GLADSTONE, William Ewart (1809-98). Four times Prime Minister and leader of the Liberal Party. He was a great orator and financier, well-known for his Irish policies concerning the disestablishment of the Church, and land and home-rule bills. His was the first state funeral since that of Pitt. His wife is also buried here.

PITT, William, the Elder, 1st Earl of Chatham (1708-78). Prime Minister and Secretary of State, 1756. He first entered parliament as an M.P. for Old Sarum. His foreign policy made England greatly respected abroad. He opposed Lord North's Government in the matter of the severance of the American colonies. He died after having a fit in the House of Lords.

STEWART, Robert, Viscount Castlereagh, later 2nd Marquess of Londonderry, K.G. (1769-1822). Leading statesman of his time. His policies, adopted at the First Congress of Vienna, led to the downfall of Napoleon. He was in favour of the enfranchisement of Irish Catholics and supported Wellesley (later Duke of Wellington) in the Napoleonic campaign. With Sidmouth, he was responsible for the Six Acts, 1819. He committed suicide, and at his funeral a riot broke out. His wife is buried in the north-east corner of the cloisters.

TEMPLE, Henry John, 3rd Viscount Palmerston, K.G. (1784-1865). Twice Prime Minister (1855-58 and 1859-65). He supported Canning and Catholic emancipation. He was a brilliant Foreign Secretary, and as Prime Minister, in 1856, promoted the Treaty of Paris. Lady Palmerston is also buried here.

VERNON, Admiral Edward (1684-1757). Nicknamed 'Old Grog' because of the grogram boat-cloak which he wore. He introduced the official rum and water ration for sailors, and the drink 'grog' is named after him.

WEST AISLE, NORTH TRANSEPT

MURRAY, William (1705-93). Created Earl of Mansfield in 1776. Lord Chief Justice of England, 1756-88. Because of his approval of the Roman Catholic Relief Bill, his Bloomsbury house was burned down by the Gordon rioters, 1780. His house at Kenwood, Highgate, was built by his friend, Robert Adam. (Monument by Flaxman)

SANDERSON, Sir William (c. 1586-1676). Historian of Mary, Queen of Scots, James I and Charles I. Gentleman of the Privy Chamber to Charles II. His wife, Bridget,

is also buried here. (Monument by Edward Marshall)

NAVE. THE UNKNOWN WARRIOR

His body was brought here from France for burial on 11th November 1920. The idea of such a burial was put forward by a chaplain at the front who noticed a grave in a garden at Armentières marked with a rough cross bearing the words 'An unknown British Soldier'. The grave in the Abbey contains soil from France and bears an inscription written by Dean Ryle.

NORTH WEST OR BELFRY TOWER

FOX, Charles James (1749-1806). A great Whig statesman. He began his career as a Tory, but went over to the Whigs at the time of the American War of Independence, 1775, and became their leader in the House of Commons. He is well-known for his opposition to Pitt and his personal friendship with the Prince of Wales. He supported Catholic emancipation and promoted the abolition of the slave trade.

WEST END OF NAVE

BURDETT-COUTTS, Angela Georgina, Baroness (1814-1906). Well known for her philanthropic work in endowing churches and schools. The first woman to be given the freedom of the city of London, 1872.

PITT, William, the Younger (1759-1806). Son of Pitt the Elder. Became Prime Minister at twenty-four and held office despite lack of support in the House of Commons. He was a great financier who took steps to reduce the national debt. He formed great coalitions against Napoleon and introduced income tax, 1798, and an Irish policy, under which the Irish and British Parliaments were united. He died, 1806, on learning of the defeat and break-up of his coalition, at Austerlitz.

ST GEORGE'S CHAPEL

ALLENBY, Edmund Henry Hynman, 1st Viscount Allenby, G.C.B. (1866-1936). Field-marshal and famous commander in the First World War. He was the officer in command when Jerusalem was recaptured.

BLANK, Bishop Joost de (1908-68). Archbishop of Cape Town, 1957-63, and Canon of Westminster, 1963-8.

SOUTH AISLE

ANDRÉ, Major John (1751-80). Adjutant-general of the British forces in America. He was engaged in secret negotiations with Benedict Arnold when he was captured, taken before General Washington as a spy, and later hanged on 2nd October 1780, aged twenty-nine. Forty years later his remains were brought from America and buried near his monument. (Monument by Adam and Gelder)

ATTERBURY, Francis (1663-1732). Famous Jacobite Dean of Westminster and Bishop of Rochester. Brilliant orator and controversial writer. He was exiled after being charged with conspiracy to place the Old Pretender on the throne, and died nine years later in Paris. He was buried in the Abbey at his own request (below the Abbot's pew)

CHAMBERLAIN, Arthur Neville (1869-1940). Statesman. Conservative Prime Minister, 1937-40, at the outbreak of the Second World War. He agreed, with Hitler, to the partition of Czechoslovakia in 1938, and believed he had averted war. Later he declared war on Germany in 1939.

LAW, Andrew Bonar (1858-1923). Statesman. Leader of the Conservative Party and Prime Minister during the last year of his life. He was a Canadian by birth, and Scottish by descent.

OLDFIELD, Ann (1683-1730). The most famous actress of her day, she was given a magnificent funeral dressed in 'a very fine Brussels lace head, a Holland shift with a tucker and double ruffles on the same lace, a pair of new kid gloves, and her body wrapped up in a winding sheet'. She is buried beneath Congreve's monument.

WADE, George (1673-1748). Field-marshal and Commander-in-Chief in Scotland during the Young Pretender's rebellion. He was responsible for the construction of some very good roads through the Highlands.

WHARTON, Henry (1664-95). Divine and author: He was famous for his ecclesiastical works, the best-known being *Anglia Sacra*. Purcell composed the anthem sung at his funeral.

NORTH AISLE

ATTLEE, Clement Richard, 1st Earl Attlee, K.G., O.M. (1883-1967). Prime Minister (1945-51) and leader of the Labour Party.

BEVIN, Ernest (1881-1951). Statesman, labour leader and trade unionist. Foreign Secretary 1945-51. He was General Secretary of the Transport and General Workers Union.

DARWIN, Charles Robert (1809-82). Naturalist and biologist. Author of the *Origin of Species,* 1859, and *The Descent of Man,* 1871, among other works.

HERSCHEL, Sir John Frederick William (1792-1871). A celebrated astronomer who discovered and catalogued many double stars and first satisfactorily measured direct solar radiation. He invented sensitized paper for photographic work.

HUNTER, John (1728-93). Surgeon and anatomist. Jenner was once his pupil. His remains were moved here from St Martin-in-the-Fields in 1859. (Buried near Ben Jonson)

JONSON, Ben (c. 1573-1637). Poet Laureate, dramatist and actor. A friend of Shakespeare and Bacon. He was buried standing on his feet, at his own request. It is said that as he was dying in poverty, he begged 'eighteen inches of square ground in Westminster Abbey' from Charles I. The body was disturbed in 1849 and it was observed that the leg bones were bolt upright in sand and the skull, which had traces of red hair on it, came rolling down from a position above the legs. His plays include *Every Man in his Humour,* 1598 (Shakespeare acted in this), *The Alchemist* and *Bartholomew Fayre.*

WEBB, Sidney James, 1st Baron Passfield (1859-1947). Economist and socialist who helped to found the Fabian Society. Together with BEATRICE, Lady Passfield (1858-1943), who is also buried here, he was involved in the founding of the *New Statesman* and wrote many books.

WOODWARD, Dr John (1665-1728). Professor of Physics at Gresham College, and author of many works on geology and natural history. He is said to have fought a duel with his fellow-doctor, Mead, over one of their numerous controversies.

CENTRE OF NAVE

BARRY, Sir Charles (1795-1860). Architect. His chief work, The Palace of Westminster (the Houses of Parliament), is pictured on the brass.

GRAHAM, George, F.R.S. (1673-1751). Mechanician who invented the mercurial pendulum and made astronomical instruments for Halley, Bradley and the French Academy. He is buried with Tompion (see below).

LIVINGSTONE, David (1813-73). Scottish explorer and missionary in Africa, where he died. He discovered the Zambezi in 1851 and died on an expedition to discover the source of the Nile. His faithful servants carried his body to Zanzibar, whence it was shipped to England.

NEWTON, Sir Isaac (1642-1727). Philosopher and mathematician, author of the *Principia,* and formulator of the law of gravity. He was President of the Royal Society for twenty-six years.

RUTHERFORD, Ernest, lst Baron (1856-1940). Physicist. He investigated radio-active transformations and the atom. He

was awarded the Nobel Prize for Chemistry in 1908.

RYLE, Herbert Edward, K.C.V.O., D.D. (1856-1925). Dean of Westminster, 1911-25. He was foremost among those responsible for the burial of the Unknown Soldier in the Abbey.

SCOTT, Sir George Gilbert (1811-78). Architect. Leader of the Gothic revival, restoring many churches throughout Great Britain, among others Ely and Salisbury Cathedrals. He also designed many new buildings—e.g., the Albert Memorial, 1864. He was made Professor of Architecture at the Royal Academy in 1868.

STEPHENSON, Robert (1803-59). Son of George Stephenson, who helped in the construction of the *Rocket.* Engineer of the Britannia Bridge, Menai Straits, and of the Birmingham Railway. Buried, by his own wish, near to Telford.

THOMSON, William, lst Baron Kelvin (1824-1907). Scientist and inventor, who took part in the laying of the Atlantic cable. He was one of the founders of the science of thermodynamics.

TOMPION, Thomas (1638-1713). 'The father of English watchmaking'. Buried in the same grave is George Graham (see above), Tompion's apprentice and friend, who succeeded to his business. Tompion invented one of the first English watches with a balance spring. He also made a clock, for the Pump-room in Bath, in 1709, which still works.

SOUTH AISLE OF CHOIR

SHOVELL, Admiral Sir Cloudesley or Clowdisley (1650-1707). The son of poor parents, he began his career as an ordinary seaman. He carried out many daring acts and rose to become Commander-of-the-Fleet. As a boy during the Dutch War of 1666-67, he carried despatches in his mouth as he swam from ship to ship under fire. In 1707 he helped to destroy the French Mediterranean Fleet at Toulon. His body was found after his ship had been wrecked off the Scilly Isles, and he was buried in Westminster Abbey. Thirty years later a fisherman's wife confessed to killing him as he lay on a rock, and stealing the valuable emerald ring which he wore on his finger. (Monument by Grinling Gibbons)

NORTH AISLE OF CHOIR

HEYLYN, Dr Peter (1600-62). Historian and author of *Cyprianus Anglicus* — i.e., 'Life of Laud', *History of the Reformation* — etc. He was Sub-dean of Westminster Abbey during Charles I's reign, and is buried beneath his Sub-dean's seat. This is in accordance with a dream he had before his last sickness, in which Charles I stood before him and said, 'Peter, I will have you buried under your seat in the church, for you are rarely seen, but there or at your study'.

SPRAGGE, Admiral Sir Edward (d.1673). As Vice-admiral he took part in a brilliant victory over the Dutch at Solebay, 1672. He was killed in action during another battle with the Dutch, 1673. His ship had been put out of action, and he was trying to reach another, when the small boat he was in was holed and sunk

WILBERFORCE, William (1759-1833). Philanthropist. M.P. for Yorkshire. He was responsible for the abolition of the African slave trade in every colony of the British Empire. He helped to found the Bible Society in 1803. (Monument by S. Joseph)

MUSICIANS' AISLE

BENNETT, Sir William Sterndale (1816-1875). Composer, Professor of Music at Cambridge and Principal of the Royal Academy of Music, London. He was a friend of Mendelssohn. He won the Beethoven gold medal from the Philharmonic Society in 1867.

BLOW, Dr John (1648-1708). Famous for his church music. He resigned as Abbey organist in favour of his young pupil, Purcell, but resumed the post on the latter's death.

CROFT, Dr William (c.1677-1727). Composer and organist of the Chapel Royal in 1707. Blow's successor as organist at the Abbey (see above).

PURCELL, Henry (c. 1658-95). One of the greatest of English composers. The whole of his short life was connected with the Abbey. Both he and his children were baptized and buried there, and he was organist at the Abbey for fourteen years. He composed music for many state occasions and his own music was played and sung at his funeral. His compositions include *Dido and Aeneas*, 1689.

STANFORD, Sir Charles Villiers (1852-1924). Composer, and Professor of Music at Cambridge. Conductor of the Bach Choir (1885-1902), and the Leeds Music Festival (1901-10).

VAUGHAN WILLIAMS, Ralph, O.M. (1872-1958). Musician and composer. Among his works are *Dona Nobis Pacem* and *Lazarus*.

SOUTH TRANSEPT

ADAM, Robert (1728-92). Famous architect, who designed and set an original style in English architecture. He was architect to George III, 1762-8. With his brothers he built the Adelphi, 1769-71.

BUSBY, Dr Richard (1606-95). The most famous schoolmaster of his time, he was Headmaster of Westminster School. One of his sayings was that the rod was his sieve and that whoever could not pass through it was no boy for him. (Buried beneath the choir)

SOUTH, Dr Robert (1634-1716). Famous preacher. He attacked Cromwell so

wittily in one of his sermons that
Charles II is said to have fallen into a fit
of uncontrollable laughter and promised
South a bishopric if he was 'put in mind
of him at the next death'. The next death,
however, was the King's own. South's
collected sermons were published and
became very popular.

POETS' CORNER

BEAUMONT, Francis (1584-1616).
Dramatist. He studied for the legal profession but later turned to writing poetry.
He became an acquaintance of Ben Jonson.
He met John Fletcher and the two wrote
plays together—a partnership which was
to make them famous. (Buried at the
entrance to St Benedict's Chapel)

BROWNING, Robert (1812-89). Poet.
He married the poetess Elizabeth Barrett
in 1846, and they lived in Italy until her
death in 1861. She was buried in Florence.
He died in Venice. The gravestone is
made from Italian marble and porphyry.
Among his best-known works are *Pippa
Passes,* 1841, and *The Ring and the
Book,* 1872.

CAMDEN, William (1551-1623). Author
and antiquary. Headmaster of Westminster
School. Author of the *Britannia,* 1586,
Annals of Queen Elizabeth and also of
the first Abbey guide-book. He founded
a Chair of History at Oxford University
in 1622.

CHAMBERS, Sir William (1726-96).
Architect of Somerset House, 1775.

CHAUCER, Geoffrey (*c.* 1343-1400).
Poet, customs officer and civil servant.
He was buried here because he was Clerk
of Works when he died. Next to Shakespeare, he has been called England's
greatest writer and poet. He was fairly
poor throughout his life, although latterly
he received royal pensions. A monument
to him was put up in 1550. His best-known
works include *Troilus and Criseyde* and
Canterbury Tales, c. 1387, first printed
by Caxton in 1475.

DICKENS, Charles (1812-70). Novelist.
His works have had perhaps the largest
circulation of any English works of fiction.
He also edited two journals, acted, and
gave readings. In spite of his request that
his body should be buried at Rochester,
or at Shorne (Kent), Dickens was given
an Abbey interment. He also requested
that no monument should be set up.
Among his many famous works are *Oliver
Twist, A Christmas Carol* and *Great
Expectations.*

DRYDEN, John (1631-1700). Poet and
satirist. Poet Laureate to Charles II and
James II. Educated at Westminster School.
In early life he was an admirer of Cromwell, but after the Restoration he became
a Royalist. He was converted to Catholicism after the accession of James II. His
works include *All for Love, Absalom and
Achitophel* and *Fables, Ancient and
Modern.*

ELIOT, Thomas Stearns, O.M. (1888-
1965). Poet and critic. Born in St Louis,
USA, he became a British citizen in 1927.
Among his best-known works are *The
Waste Land* and *Murder in the Cathedral.*
He was awarded the Nobel Prize for
Literature in 1948.

GARRICK, David (1717-79). Very famous
actor-manager and playwright. He was a
pupil of Dr Johnson who came to London
with him. His funeral procession stretched
from his house in the Adelphi to the
Abbey, and included many celebrated
literary figures. Garrick's wife is buried in
the same grave.

GAY, John (1685-1732). Poet and
dramatist. He was sponsored by Swift and
Pope. Gay's chief dramatic work was *The
Beggar's Opera,* which was revived in 1920.
Hogarth painted scenes from the original
production.

HAKLUYT, Richard (*c.* 1552-1616).
Geographer, known as the 'father of
modern geographers'. His *Principall
Navigations, Voiages and Discoveries of
the English Nation* was published in 1589.

HANDEL, George Frederick (1685-1759). Musical composer. He was born in Saxony and studied music at Halle. After work as a conductor in Hamburg, he composed his first opera *Almira,* 1705. He came to England from Italy in 1710, and his opera *Rinaldo* was produced at the Queen's Theatre, Haymarket. He settled in England after 1712 and was appointed Court Composer by George I, producing many operas and composing music for the Church. In 1737 he became partially paralysed. His oratorio the *Messiah* was composed in twenty-three days and first performed in Dublin in 1741. He is most famous for his choral works.

HARDY, Thomas (1840-1928). Novelist and poet who wrote about his native Wessex. His ashes are buried near those of Dickens, and his heart lies in the family tomb in Stinsford Churchyard. Among his many novels are *Far from the Madding Crowd, Tess of the d'Urbervilles* and *Jude the Obscure.*

HAULE, Robert (d. 1378). Murdered by the followers of John of Gaunt in the choir where he had taken sanctuary. After this act the Abbey was closed for four months, until sanctuary rights were freshly decreed. His friend, John SHAKEL, who escaped from the killers, was buried in the same grave in 1396.

HEATHER, or HEYTHER, William (c. 1563-1627). Musical composer, chorister and lay vicar in the Abbey choir. He founded the music lectureship at Oxford which bears his name.

IRVING, Sir Henry (1838-1905). His original name was John Henry Brodribb. Actor-manager. He revolutionized the art of drama with his revivals of Shakespeare's plays at the Lyceum Theatre, 1878-99.

JOHNSON, Dr Samuel (1709-84). Lexicographer and writer. After his education at Oxford he became a schoolmaster and came to London with his pupil, Garrick, in 1737. He suffered much ill-health and poverty. He edited *The Rambler* and his

other famous works include the *Dictionary of the English Language, Rasselas, Lives of the Poets* and *Journey to the Western Isles of Scotland.* He founded the Ivy Lane and Literary Clubs and was a great conversationalist, immortalized by Boswell in his writings.

KIPLING, Rudyard (1865-1936). Author and poet. Many of his stories were set in India. Among his works are *The Jungle Book, Puck of Pook's Hill* and *Barrack-Room Ballads.*

LITLYNGTON or LITTLINGTON, Abbot Nicholas (c. 1316-86). He rebuilt the west and south cloister and part of the Abbot's lodgings, including the Jerusalem Chamber and the College Hall. He assisted at the coronation of Richard II in 1377.

MASEFIELD, John, O.M. (1878-1967). Author and Poet Laureate, 1930-67. He ran away to sea at the age of thirteen and many of his works are about the sea—e.g., *Salt Water Ballads,* 1902.

MORAY, Sir Robert (1603-73). Soldier, chemist and mathematician. One of the founders of the Royal Society and its first President.

MURRAY, Gilbert, O.M. (1866-1957). Classical scholar and historian.

PARR, Thomas (c. 1483-1635 aged 152 years). Lived in Alderbury, near Shrewsbury. It is thought that he lived through ten reigns. His portrait was painted by Van Dyck.

PRIOR, Matthew (1664-1721). Poet and diplomat. He held several offices under William III. He went to Paris to negotiate for the Treaty of Utrecht, 1713, which was known as 'Matt's peace'. Among his works are *The Town and Country Mouse* and *To a Child of Quality.* (Buried at the feet of Spenser)

SHERIDAN, Richard Brinsley (1751-1816). Parliamentary orator and dramatist. Author of *The Rivals* and *The School for Scandal*. His fame came too late and he is said to have died in poverty, his financial rewards serving only to give him a magnificent funeral.

SPENSER, Edmund (*c.* 1552-99). Poet. Author of the *Shepheardes Calender* and the *Faerie Queene,* which he dedicated to Queen Elizabeth I. He was Lord Deputy of Ireland in 1580. Later he had to flee Ireland when his home was burned in an insurrection in 1598. He was said to have died of starvation. Shakespeare attended his funeral.

TENNYSON, Alfred, Lord (1809-92). Poet. He succeeded Wordsworth as Poet Laureate in 1850. Among his most famous works are *In Memoriam, Idylls of the King* and *Maud.*

WARD, Dr Joshua (1686-1761). Celebrated chemist and quack doctor. Inventor of the medicine, Friar's Balsam. He founded a hospital in Westminster. George II, Hogarth and Fielding were among his patients.

WYATT, James (1746-1813). Architect, and surveyor of the Abbey, 1776. He was given the name 'Destroyer' for misdirecting his love of Gothic architecture to the restoration of English buildings.

CHOIR AND SANCTUARY

ANNE of CLEVES (1515-57). Fourth wife of Henry VIII. After her divorce from him, she lived in Chelsea on a royal pension. She died a Roman Catholic. The decoration (a skull and crossbones design) on the marble slab over her tomb is said to be the earliest of its kind in England and was placed there in 1606.

CROUCHBACK, Edmund, Earl of Lancaster (1245-96). The second son of Henry III, who was made Duke of Lancaster in 1267. He was given the title, King of Sicily, by the Pope although he later renounced this. In 1269 he married Aveline de Forz (see below), and after her death, Blanche, widow of Henry of Navarre. He commanded the English Army, without success, in Gascony in 1296.

DE FORZ, Aveline, Countess of Lancaster (d. 1274). Wife of Edmund Crouchback. An heiress to a considerable fortune, she died childless, and her wealth endowed the future House of Lancaster. (Buried near her husband)

NEVILLE, Queen Anne (1456-85). Wife of Richard III, and daughter of Warwick 'the King-maker'. (Unmarked grave)

VALENCE, Aymer de, Earl of Pembroke (1270-1324). Son of William de Valence

Anne of Cleves

(see page 62). He was Guardian of Scotland from 1306-7, where he captured, and put to death, Nigel, brother of Robert Bruce. He won the Battle of Ruthven, 1306, and fought at Bannockburn, 1314.

South Ambulatory

SEBERT or SABA, (d. circa 616). First Christian King of Essex, converted by Bishop Mellitus. The traditional founder of the Abbey. His tomb is reputed to contain the bones of his Queen, ETHELGODA.

TOUNSON, TOWNSON or TOULSON, Robert (1575-1621). Dean of Westminster 1617, then Bishop of Salisbury. It was during Tounson's period at Westminster that Sir Walter Raleigh was imprisoned in the old Gatehouse, which was once the old monastery prison. Tounson prayed with Raleigh the night before his execution, and was amazed at the gaiety and courage with which he faced death.

CHAPEL OF ST BENEDICT

LANGHAM, Simon de (d. 1376). Abbot of Westminster from 1349-60. He was made Lord Chancellor of England and then appointed Archbishop of Canterbury by Edward III, the only Westminster Abbot to attain this position. He died at Avignon, but was buried in the Abbey at his own request.

SPOTTISWOODE or SPOTSWOOD, John (1565-1639). Archbishop of St Andrews, 1615, and historian of the Scottish Church. Charles I was crowned King of Scotland by him. He promoted the Five Articles of Perth, in 1618, and was deposed for trying to modify Charles I's policy on the introduction of the liturgy in 1637.

VINCENT, William (1739-1815). Headmaster of Westminster School and Dean of Westminster. He purchased land in Tothill Fields for a boys' playground, which was called Vincent Square after him.

BETWEEN THE CHAPEL OF ST BENEDICT AND THE CHAPEL OF ST EDMUND

BERKYNG, Richard (d. 1246). Abbot of Westminster from 1222. One of the witnesses at the signing of the Magna Carta and a favourite of Henry III. (Exact position of grave not known)

Children of Henry III: KATHERINE (d. 1257, aged 5 years), also four other children. Katherine was dumb but very beautiful. Her death was a great grief to Henry who ordered a richly decorated monument for her. Traces of the mosaic work can be seen today. Also in the same grave are four of the children of Edward I.

CHAPEL OF ST EDMUND

BLANCHE OF THE TOWER (d. 1340). One of the children of Edward III. Her name derives from the place of her birth. She is buried beside WILLIAM WINDSOR (see below).

BOURCHIER, Sir Humphrey (d.1471). He was killed fighting for Edward IV at the Battle of Barnet. (His helmet with crest, etc., still exists)

CLIFFORD, Margaret, Countess of Derby (d. 1596). The sister of Frances, Duchess of Suffolk (see above). She was imprisoned for witchcraft by her jealous cousin, Queen Elizabeth, in 1590.

GREY, Frances, Duchess of Suffolk (1517-59). Daughter of Charles Brandon, Duke of Suffolk, and mother of Lady Jane Grey. Her funeral was the first Protestant service held in the Abbey after the reconstitution of the chapter by Queen Elizabeth.

HOLLES, Sir Frescheville (1641-72). Hero in naval battles with the Dutch off Lowestoft. He was killed in the battle of Solebay.

JOHN of ELTHAM, Earl of Cornwall (1316-36). The second son of Edward II, and Regent of the Kingdom during his brother, Edward III's, absence. He was prominent in quelling border raids by the Scots. He died at Perth, aged nineteen.

VALENCE, William de, Lord of Pembroke and Wexford (d. 1296). Half-brother of Henry III. He went on Crusade with Edward I in 1270. (Interesting tomb decorated with Limoges champlevé enamelwork)

WALDBY or WALDEBY, Robert de (d.1398). Archbishop of York. Friend and adviser to the Black Prince.

WILLIAM WINDSOR and BLANCHE OF THE TOWER (d. 1340). The two children of Edward III. Their surnames derive from the place of their birth.

CHAPEL OF ST NICHOLAS

ELIZABETH, Duchess of Northumberland (d. 1776). Her funeral was the scene of great uproar, the crowd breaking down the canopy of John of Eltham's tomb and several people being injured. The burial service had to be postponed until after midnight.

PHILIPPA, Duchess of York (d. 1431). Wife of the second Duke of York (grandson of Edward III). She held the lordship of the Isle of Wight after her husband's death.

VILLIERS, George (d. 1606). Father of George Villiers, Duke of Buckingham (see page 64). His ghost is supposed to have appeared at the bedside of his son's servant, telling him to warn his son of the extreme malice directed against him by the people.

WINIFRED, Marchioness of Winchester (d. 1586). Daughter of Sir John Bridges, Lieutenant of the Tower, she attended Lady Jane Grey on the scaffold and received, as a gift, her prayer book (now in the British Museum).

CHAPEL OF HENRY VII

ANNE, Duchess of York (1637-71). First wife of James II and mother of Queens, Mary and Anne.

DOUGLAS, Margaret, Countess of Lennox (1515-78). Daughter of Margaret Tudor, who was the widow of James IV of Scotland. She died in poverty in Hackney, and was buried in the Abbey by order of her cousin, Elizabeth I. She was the mother of Lord Darnley.

ELIZABETH, Queen of Bohemia (1596-1662). The daughter of James I and VI and wife of Frederick V, Elector Palatine.

MARY, Queen of Scots (1542-87). Daughter of James V of Scotland. She first married the French Dauphin—later Francis II—and lived in France until his death in 1560. She returned to Scotland where she married Lord Darnley, the father of her son, James I of England, and when he died (in suspicious circumstances) she married the Earl of Bothwell. This marriage was unpopular with the Scottish Lords who defeated Mary at the Battle of Langside in 1568. A fervent Roman Catholic with a strong claim to the English throne, Mary was Elizabeth I's deadliest rival; however, she sought sanctuary in England, where she was arrested, and after nineteen years in prison executed at Fotheringhay Castle. She was first buried in Peterborough Cathedral, but her body was transferred to the Abbey by her son, James I, and now lies opposite that of her cousin Elizabeth I.

RUPERT, Prince (1619-82). Count Palatine of Rhine and Duke of Bavaria. The son of Elizabeth of Bohemia (see above). He fought for Charles I at Edgehill and Marston Moor. Later he fought at sea against the Dutch and became First Lord of the Admiralty in 1673. He was the founder of the Hudson Bay Company in 1670.

STANLEY, Margaret, Countess of Richmond and Derby (1443-1509). Best known as Lady Margaret Beaufort. She was the mother of Henry VII by her second husband, Edmund Tudor (she was married four times). She is well-remembered as the founder of two Cambridge colleges—Christ's and St John's. She was also the patroness of Caxton and Wynkyn de Worde.

SOUTH AISLE

STUART, Lady Arabella (1575-1615). Daughter of Charles, Earl of Lennox. Because of her connection through marriage to the Suffolk branch of the royal family, James I regarded her as a dangerous claimant to the throne and had her imprisoned in the Tower, where she lost her reason and died in a few years. Her body was brought to the Abbey at midnight and buried without solemnity on the coffin of her aunt, Mary, Queen of Scots.

WILLIAM, Duke of Gloucester, who died in 1700 aged eleven. He is said to have developed a fever through 'excessive dancing on his birthday'.

IN THE VAULT BELOW THE NAVE OF THE CHAPEL OF HENRY VII

ANNE, Queen (1665-1714). Second daughter of James II by his first wife, Lady Anne Hyde. She had to be carried to her coronation from St James's Palace, owing to an attack of gout. During her reign the Act of Union with Scotland was passed in 1707.
Also her husband PRINCE GEORGE of Denmark (1653-1707) and their many infants. George was refused the title of king but named Generalissimo, 1702.

CHARLES II (1630-85). Son of Charles I, who returned to England from exile at the Restoration of 1660. His reign was regarded as dissolute and frivolous and his policy of toleration towards the Catholics made him unpopular. He had several mistresses the most famous of whom was

Nell Gwyn. Although his coronation was magnificent, his funeral took place at night without ceremony. He acknowledged himself a Catholic on his deathbed.

MARY II, Queen (1662-94). Crowned with her husband, William, Prince of Orange, in the Abbey in 1689. She died of smallpox at Hampton Court. Both Houses of Parliament attended her funeral—a departure from tradition, for until then Parliament had always 'expired with the Sovereign'.

WILLIAM III, Prince of Orange (1650-1702). Grandson of Charles I, born at The Hague. He founded Greenwich Hospital in memory of his wife, Mary II (see above). He championed Protestantism and he defeated James II at the Boyne, becoming King when Mary's right to succession was established. In 1701 he agreed to the Act of Settlement which secured the succession for the House of Hanover.

NAVE OF THE CHAPEL

CAROLINE, of Anspach (1683-1737). Consort of George II (they are buried together). Handel composed the anthem 'When the ear heard her, then it blessed her' for her funeral. She exerted considerable influence over her husband and completely supported Walpole. She had an intense hatred of her son, Frederick.

EDWARD VI (1537-53). Son of Henry VIII and Jane Seymour. He authorized the publication of the first English Prayer Book, compiled by Cranmer, and the burial service was used for the first time over a sovereign at his funeral.

ELIZABETH of York (1465-1503). Eldest daughter of Edward IV, and as Henry VII's queen, the last of the House of York to wear the crown. She died in the Tower. Her death was, in part, due to grief at the death of her son, Arthur.

GEORGE II (1683-1760). Elector of Hanover, crowned King of England in 1727. He suppressed the Jacobite

Rebellion of 1745 in Scotland. During his reign Britain was successful in campaigns in India and Canada.

HENRY VII (1457-1509). Son of Margaret Beaufort and Edmund Tudor. It is said that Richard III's crown was placed on Henry's head at the Battle of Bosworth Field in 1485. He was later crowned in the Abbey. He was considered one of the wisest princes of his time, especially in commercial and financial affairs.

JAMES I (1566-1625). Son of Mary, Queen of Scots. He succeeded to the Scottish Throne as James VI, and on Elizabeth I's death was crowned King of England, thereby uniting both countries. Although not a heroic figure he was a very learned and good king. His exact burial place in the Abbey was not determined until 1869.

WILLIAM AUGUSTUS, Duke of Cumberland (1721-65). Third son of George II. He was for some time Commander-in-Chief of the British forces, and was named the 'Butcher of Culloden' for the brutal way in which he put down the '45 Rebellion of the Jacobites. Later he fell out of favour with his father when he was defeated by the French at Hastenbeck, 1757. He was keen on horse-racing and founded the meeting at Ascot.

RAF CHAPEL

CATHERINE, Duchess of Buckinghamshire (d. 1743). Illegitimate daughter of James II. She planned her own funeral in detail: her ladies in waiting were made to promise that if she were to become unconscious in their presence, they would stand up until she was dead.

CLAYPOLE or CLAYPOOLE, Elizabeth (d. 1658). Oliver Cromwell's second and favourite daughter.

CROMWELL, Oliver (1599-1658). The Protector who defeated the Royalists and promoted the execution of Charles I. He was buried in the Abbey, but disinterred in 1661 and hung on a gallows at Tyburn on 30th January 1661, the twelfth anniversary of King Charles's execution. His head was put on a pole on top of Westminster Hall; his trunk was buried under the gallows. It was said that this was not his body, but that it had been secretly buried at night in the battlefield of Naseby.

DOWDING, Sir Hugh Caswall, 1st Baron Dowding (1882-1970). Commander of the RAF fighter forces during the Battle of Britain.

SHEFFIELD, John, 1st Duke of Buckingham (1648-1721). He had a very distinguished political and military career under Charles II, but was banished from Court for courting Princess Anne, who later restored him on her accession. He promoted the invitation of the Electress Sophia to England. He was a friend of Pope and patron of Dryden.

TRENCHARD, Hugh Montague, 1st Viscount Trenchard (1873-1956). Marshal of the Royal Air Force, 1927.

VILLIERS, George, 1st Duke of Buckingham (1592-1628). Son of George Villiers (see page 62). He was a great favourite of James I and Charles I, but his bad counsel and rash thinking made him unpopular with nation and Parliament. He was assassinated in Portsmouth by a soldier.

NORTH AISLE

ADDISON, Joseph (1672-1719). The first of the English essayists, called 'the noblest purifier of English literature'. He was famous for his essays in the Whig *Spectator*. The funeral took place at dead of night, the procession by torchlight passing round the shrine of St Edward and the graves of the Plantagenets to the Chapel of Henry VII. (Monument in Poets' Corner)

ELIZABETH I (1533-1603). Queen of England. Daughter of Henry VIII and Anne Boleyn and considered illegitimate by the Catholic Church. Her long reign is regarded as one of the most brilliant in English history, and at her death she was greatly mourned.

MARY TUDOR (1516-58). Half-sister to Elizabeth I, being the daughter of Catherine of Aragon. She married her cousin, Philip of Spain, but the marriage was not a success. Her devotion to the Catholic Church caused great persecution of Protestants, for which she is remembered as 'Bloody Mary'. The last requiem mass said at the Abbey was on the occasion of her funeral. The inscription says 'Consorts both in throne and grave, here rest we two sisters, Elizabeth and Mary, in the hope of one resurrection'.

INNOCENTS' CORNER

Here lie the bones taken from the Tower by Charles II and reputed to belong to the two Princes, allegedly murdered by their uncle Richard III in 1483 (according to Sir Thomas More). They were Edward V (b. 1470) and Richard, Duke of York (b. 1472).

NORTH AMBULATORY

BERKELEY, Admiral Sir William (1638-65). Lieutenant-governor of Portsmouth, 1665. He was killed in a bloody battle with the Dutch off North Foreland. The Dutch paid great tribute to him by carrying his body on his own ship, the *Swiftsure,* to Holland where it was placed in the cathedral at The Hague. It was later sent to the Abbey for interment, at the request of the Berkeley family.

ESTENEY, John (d. 1498). Abbot of Westminster from 1474 until his death. He was the guardian of Elizabeth Woodville when she sought sanctuary there with her daughter in 1483. He was also Caxton's patron and permitted him to set up his press within the Abbey

precincts. Esteney's tomb was moved and mutilated in the eighteenth century. In 1772 it was opened and the Abbot's body was found lying in a quilted chest, robed in a gown of crimson silk.

HYDE, Edward, 1st Earl of Clarendon (1609-74). Statesman, and historian of the Civil Wars and the Restoration period. He was a Royalist who was a legal adviser to Charles I and was later Lord Chancellor to Charles II, 1658. Died an exile in Rouen. He was the grandfather of Queens Mary and Anne.

JOHN LOUIS, 1st Earl Ligonier of Ripley (1680-1770). Field-marshal, 1766. A French refugee who served under Marlborough at the Battle of Blenheim, 1704. Later he was Commander-in-Chief in the Austrian Netherlands, 1746-7. (Moore sculpture)

CHAPEL OF ST PAUL

BROMLEY, Sir Thomas (1530-87). Lord Chancellor. He presided at the trial of Mary, Queen of Scots, in 1586, and never recovered from this responsibility, dying two months after her execution.

HILL, Sir Rowland (1795-1879). Inventor of the penny postage and a rotary printing press. As Chairman of the Brighton Railway, 1843-6, he introduced express and excursion trains. He received the freedom of the City of London in 1879.

PUCKERING, Sir John (1544-96). Lord Keeper of the Great Seal and, twice Speaker of the House of Commons. He took an active part in the trial of Mary, Queen of Scots, and later, at Queen Elizabeth's wish, prosecuted his secretary, Davison, for obtaining her signature on the death warrant.

ST JOHN THE BAPTIST'S CHAPEL

CAREY, Thomas (d. 1649). Gentleman of the Bedchamber to Charles I. He is said to have died of grief at Charles's death.

COLCHESTER, William de (d. 1420). Abbot of Westminster. He was committed to the Tower for a period in 1400 because of his involvement in a plot to restore Richard II, but came back into favour under Henry V.

DEVEREUX, Robert, 3rd Earl of Essex (1591-1646). The son of Elizabeth I's favourite. He served under Charles I, but went over to the Parliamentarians in 1642. He was General of the Parliamentarian army in 1642 at Edgehill, but he later resigned in disagreement with Cromwell's Scottish policy.

MILLYNG, Thomas (d. 1492). Abbot of Westminster, 1469-74. During this time Elizabeth Woodville first took sanctuary at the Abbey, and her son, Edward V, was born in the Abbot's house. Edward IV gave him the Bishopric of Hereford in 1474 as a reward for this protection of the Queen.

RUTHALL or ROWTHALL, Thomas (d. 1523). Bishop of Durham. Private Secretary to Henry VII and Privy Councillor to Henry VIII. Keeper of the Privy Seal, 1516.

VAUGHAN, Sir Thomas (d. 1483). Private Treasurer to Edward IV, then Chamberlain to his son Edward V. He was beheaded on the order of Richard III, at Pontefract, after Edward V's death.

ISLIP CHANTRY CHAPEL

ISLIP, John (1464-1532). Abbot of Westminster from 1500. Born at Islip, Oxfordshire. He was a favourite of Henry VII and Henry VIII, and a Privy Councillor. Islip was called 'the great builder' because of the part which he played in the building of the Abbey. It was under his direction that Henry VII's Chapel was built, and also the chapel known by his own name.

CHAPEL OF ST JOHN THE EVANGELIST

VERE, Sir Francis (1560-1609). A great soldier during the reign of Elizabeth.

Commander-in-Chief of the English forces in the Netherlands in 1598, where he gained great honour by his courage against the Spaniards. He was Governor of Portsmouth in 1606. His account of his service, *Commentaries,* was published in 1657.

ST ANDREW'S CHAPEL

TELFORD, Thomas (1757-1834). Known in his time as the 'first engineer in Europe'. He was a founder member of the Institute of Civil Engineers, 1818, and was its first President. He designed the Menai Bridge and the Caledonian Canal. His autobiography was published in 1838.

CHAPEL OF ST EDWARD THE CONFESSOR

ALMAYNE, Henry d' (d. 1271). Son of Richard, King of the Romans, and nephew of Henry III. He was murdered in the cathedral at Viterbo by the sons of Simon de Montfort. His heart was preserved for a long time in a golden cup near the Shrine of Edward the Confessor.

CATHERINE of VALOIS (1401-37). Queen to Henry V and, after his death, wife to Owen Tudor. She died in a monastery at Bermondsey, and was buried with much pomp in the Abbey. Her body was later moved to an open coffin near Henry V's tomb, where it remained for over two hundred years. Pepys wrote, in 1669, that he had seen the body in this coffin and that he kissed the mouth of a queen on his thirty-sixth birthday.

EADGYTH or MATILDA (1080-1118). Wife of Henry I. Her marriage with him united the Saxon and Norman peoples. Noted for her extreme piety, she would walk every day in Lent from the Palace to the Abbey barefoot and wearing sackcloth, and would kiss the feet of the poorest people and give them alms. She built a leper hospital at St Giles-in-the-Fields.

EDITH or the Lady Eadgyth (d. 1075). Wife of Edward the Confessor and daughter of Earl Godwine of Essex. She was very beautiful, renowned for her learning, and 'a lady of singular piety and sweet modesty'. On Edward's death he asked her to support her brother, Harold, whom she did, in fact, desert in 1066.

EDWARD THE CONFESSOR (*c.* 1002-66). He reigned 1042-66. He was very pious and did not care for affairs of state, but was worshipped as a saint by his people. The Abbey was built at his instigation, fulfilling a promise which he had made to the Pope as absolution for breaking his vow to make a pilgrimage to Rome. Many miracles are said to have taken place near the tomb. In 1102 the tomb was opened in the presence of Henry I and the body was found to be as flexible as if he were asleep. He was canonized in 1161.

EDWARD I 'Longshanks' (1239-1307). The first king to be crowned in the Abbey as it is now. Like his father, Henry III, he was a benefactor of the Abbey, and deposited, in the Shrine of St Edward, the Stone of Scone and the Scottish regalia. He fought campaigns in France, Wales and Scotland and laid down much legislation, including many harsh measures—e.g. the expulsion of the Jews, 1290. Died on a Scottish campaign.

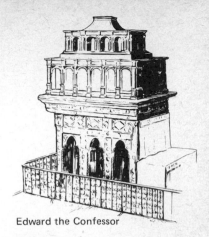
Edward the Confessor

EDWARD III (1312-77). Son of Edward II and Isabel, he reigned for fifty years and during this time exerted English influence in both Scotland and France, and kept David II of Scotland a prisoner for many years. After the death of his son, the Black Prince, he was overcome with grief, lost all interest in life, and died, attended only by one poor priest. He founded the order of the Garter, *c.* 1349, and encouraged Flemish weavers to settle in England. He forbade the payment of Peter's pence to the Pope.

ELEANOR, of Castile (d. 1290). First wife of Edward I, whom she accompanied on crusade to the Holy Land, 1270. It is said that she saved his life there by sucking

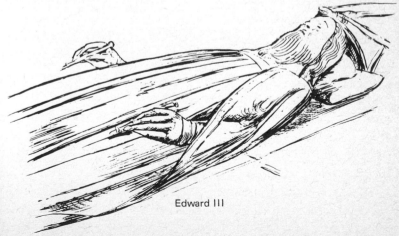
Edward III

the poison from a wound made by an assassin's dagger. She died in Harby (Nottinghamshire) and Edward brought her body to Westminster, erecting memorial crosses at the places where the procession rested on the way.

HENRY III (1207-72). Builder of the greater part of the present church. Henry was very extravagant; he built the Abbey with money extracted from his people, but was finally forced to pawn the jewels with which he had enriched the Shrine of St Edward. After his death his heart was delivered to the Abbess of Fontevrault. to be placed in the Norman abbey where his family were buried. Throughout his reign he quarrelled with the Pope, other Powers and his nobles, in particular Simon de Montfort, all of which drained his resources in what might otherwise have been a very successful reign.

HENRY V (1388-1422). Eldest son of Henry IV, whom he succeeded in 1413. He was an excellent king and a popular hero, particularly after his success at the Battle of Agincourt, 1415.

PHILIPPA of Hainault (c. 1314-69). Wife of Edward III, in whose absence she defended the kingdom against the Scots. In 1347 she interceded with Edward III for the lives of the six burghers of Calais. Her last wish was that her husband should be buried next to her on his death.

RICHARD II (1367-1400). Son of the Black Prince and King from 1377 to 1399. He showed great courage as a boy of fourteen, when he quelled the rebellion, led by Wat Tyler, at Smithfield. Nevertheless, Richard was a weak ruler and was eventually deposed by his cousin, Henry Bolingbroke, and murdered at Pontefract Castle. (Also buried here is his first wife, ANNE of Bohemia)

THOMAS of Woodstock, Earl of Buckingham and Duke of Gloucester (1355-97). The youngest son of Edward III and Philippa of Hainault. He was

created Duke of Gloucester by Richard II, who later accused him of conspiring against the Crown. He was taken to Calais where he was smothered under a feather mattress.

TUDOR, Princess Elizabeth (d. 1495). Daughter of Henry VII. She died at the age of three and was given a magnificent funeral, her body being carried to the Abbey in a black 'chair' drawn from Eltham by six horses.

CLOISTERS   EAST WALK

BEHN, Aphra (1640-89). The only woman dramatist and novelist buried at Westminster Abbey. She was employed by Charles II as a political spy at Antwerp in 1666 and it was she who warned that the Dutch planned to sail up the Thames. Her warning was not heeded, however, and the attack took place.

BETTERTON, Thomas (c. 1635-1710). Actor. He was the son of a cook in Charles I's kitchen. Considered the best tragedian of his time, Betterton's greatest performance was as Hamlet in 1661. His wife, BESS SANDERSON, who is buried in the same grave, took the part of Ophelia.

HUMFREY, Pelham (1647-74). Famous musician and composer of many anthems and secular songs. He was Purcell's tutor, and held jointly with him the patent of Lutenist to King Charles II.

TROUTBECK, Dr John (1832-99). Chaplain in Ordinary to Queen Victoria. He superintended many special services at the Abbey, including Queen Victoria's Diamond Jubilee. Troutbeck also translated the words to much of Bach's Passion music.

ENTRANCE TO CHAPTER HOUSE

EDWIN, Abbot (1049-71). Friend and adviser of Edward the Confessor and first Abbot of Westminster.

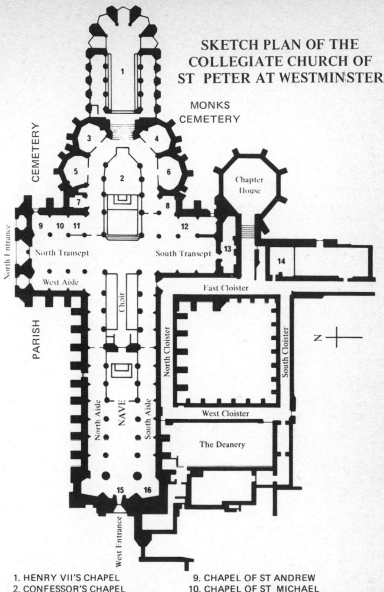

SKETCH PLAN OF THE COLLEGIATE CHURCH OF ST PETER AT WESTMINSTER

MONKS CEMETERY

CEMETERY

North Entrance

North Transept

South Transept

Chapter House

West Aisle

East Cloister

PARISH

Choir

North Cloister

South Cloister

N

West Cloister

NAVE

North Aisle

South Aisle

The Deanery

West Entrance

1. HENRY VII'S CHAPEL
2. CONFESSOR'S CHAPEL
3. CHAPEL OF ST PAUL
4. CHAPEL OF ST NICHOLAS
5. CHAPEL OF ST JOHN THE BAPTIST
6. CHAPEL OF ST EDMUND
7. ISLIP CHANTRY CHAPEL
8. CHAPEL OF ST BENEDICT
9. CHAPEL OF ST ANDREW
10. CHAPEL OF ST MICHAEL
11. CHAPEL OF ST JOHN THE EVANGELIST
12. POETS' CORNER
13. ST FAITH'S CHAPEL
14. CHAPEL OF THE PYX
15. UNKNOWN WARRIOR
16. ST GEORGE'S CHAPEL

SKETCH BASED ON OFFICIAL WESTMINSTER ABBEY PLAN

Victoria Street

WESTMINSTER CATHEDRAL *(Ashley Place)*

Underground: Victoria   Buses: 11, 24, 29

The Cathedral stands on the ground of Tothill Fields Prison. In 1883 it was purchased by Cardinal Manning, the architect was J. F. Bentley and it is in the early Christian Byzantine style.

BENCKENDORFF, Alexander or Aleksandr Konstantinovich, Count (1849-1917). Diplomat and Russian Ambassador in London, 1903-16. He helped to form the Triple Entente of 1907.

CHALLONER, Richard (1691-1781). Roman Catholic priest and philosopher.

GODFREY, William, Cardinal (1889-1963). Archbishop of Westminster, 1956-63.

GRIFFIN, Bernard, Cardinal (1899-1956). Archbishop of Westminster, 1943-56.

HINSLEY, Arthur, Cardinal (1865-1943). Archbishop of Westminster, 1935-43.

MANNING, Henry Edward, Cardinal (1808-92). At first an Archdeacon in the Church of England, he joined the Roman Catholic Church in 1851 and became Archbishop of Westminster in 1865. His body was transferred from Kensal Green to a tomb in the Cathedral crypt.

SOUTHWORTH, John (1592-1654). After training for the priesthood he worked among the poor in Westminster. He was arrested for treason and hanged, drawn and quartered at Tyburn. His remains were smuggled to France, but brought back to England at the time of the Revolution and buried there. He was later beatified, 1929, and transferred to the Cathedral in May 1930.

ST PANCRAS OLD CHURCH ▷

CAMBERWELL

Church Street

ST GILES

Buses: 12, 36, 171

The present church was designed by Sir Gilbert Scott and built on the site of an earlier church which burned down in 1841. Mary Wesley, wife of John Wesley, lies under the main roadway.

BROWN, Timothy (1744-1820). 'Equality Brown'. A partisan of Queen Caroline.

MAJOR, Thomas (1720-99). Engraver. He worked in Paris, and on his return to England he issued a series of prints (1754). He was engraver to the King and to the Stamp Office, and the first engraver to be elected as an A.R.A., 1770.

PARR, Richard (1617-91). Vicar of Reigate and Camberwell, who published a Life of James Ussher, Archbishop of Armagh, whose chaplain he had been in Cardiff in 1644.

WARNER, Lucy (1750-1821). She was only thirty-two inches in height and kept a very successful school.

CHELSEA

Church Street   CHELSEA OLD CHURCH, ALL SAINTS OR ST LUKE'S

Buses: 39, 137

The church was probably founded in the twelfth or thirteenth century. Before it was destroyed in 1941, it contained several styles of architecture, the oldest parts being the chancel and two chapels, only one of which still survives. This is the one built by Sir Thomas More to contain his tomb. He worshipped here and came to this church for confession on the morning of his trial. Amongst those buried here—Sir John Fielding, Sir Hans Sloane and Sir Thomas More's daughter, Margaret.

BOYER, Abel (1667-1729). French teacher to William, Duke of Gloucester, the only child of Queen Anne to survive infancy. He was the publisher of a periodical, the *Political State of Great Britain.*

FIELDING, Sir John (d. 1780). Magistrate who was blind from birth. Half-brother to Henry Fielding, the novelist. He began schemes for sending distressed boys into the Royal Navy, and helping deserted girls.

FLETCHER, Elizabeth (d. 1592). First wife of Bishop Richard Fletcher, and mother of John Fletcher, the poet and dramatist.

HERBERT, Magdalen (*c.* 1568-1627). Mother of George Herbert and of Lord

Herbert of Cherbury. Izaak Walton attended her funeral in the church. She was a good friend of John Donne and a very pious woman who took a great interest in the education of her ten children.

KENRICK, William (*c.* 1725-79). A writer who libelled almost all of the successful actors and authors of his day, including Goldsmith, Garrick, Fielding and Johnson.

MOSSOP, Henry (*c.* 1729-*c.* 74). An actor who appeared with Garrick in London. He was arrested for debt in 1771.

ROPER, Margaret (1505-44). Daughter of Sir Thomas More. She privately purchased her father's head, after it had been stuck on London Bridge, and

72

preserved it until her death. A head, presumed to be that of Sir Thomas More, was found in a lead box in the Roper vault, in St Dunstan's, Canterbury, in 1824.

SHADWELL, Thomas (c. 1642-92). Dramatist and poet. He frequently satirized Dryden, whom he succeeded as Poet Laureate.

SLOANE, Sir Hans (1660-1753). Physician to Queen Anne and to George II and President of the Royal College of Physicians. (Monument survives in the churchyard)

WOODFALL, Henry Sampson (1739-1805). Printer and journalist. He was Master of the Stationers' Company, 1797, and printer of the *Public Advertiser*, etc.

CHISWICK

Chiswick Mall

ST NICHOLAS'S CHURCH

Buses: 27

The early church, from which the old tower still remains, goes back to the fifteenth century. The present church was built in 1884. Among those buried in the churchyard are William Hogarth and his wife, Lady Castlemaine and William Kent.

BRIGHT, Sir Charles Tilston (1832-88). Engineer. He laid the first Atlantic cable from Valentia to Newfoundland and was one of the founders of the Atlantic Telegraph Company. He was only twenty-six years of age when he was knighted.

CARY, Rev. Henry Francis (1772-1844). Translator, notably of Pindar and of Dante's *Divine Comedy*.

CHARDIN, Sir John (1643-1713). Jeweller who travelled to Turkey, Persia and India. He was born in Paris, but came to England in 1681 because he was persecuted as a Protestant in France. An account of his travels in Persia was published in 1671.

CORBET, Miles (d. 1662). Barrister and M.P. for Great Yarmouth. He signed Charles I's death warrant in 1649, was arrested in Holland after the Restoration and executed in London.

FAUCONBERG, Mary, Countess (c. 1636-1712). Cromwell's third daughter.

HOGARTH, William (1697-1764). Painter and engraver. Famous for his series of engravings—e.g. *The Rake's Progress*. He disliked foreigners, and attacked art critics for neglecting native talent. His

wife, Jane THORNHILL (1709-89) (daughter of the painter) is also buried here.

HOLLAND, Charles (1733-69). Actor. He appeared at Drury Lane and was much praised for his acting by Chatterton, although Charles Churchill satirized him. The inscription was written by Garrick, who was his friend. (Family vault in the churchyard)

William Hogarth

KENT, William (1684-1748). Painter, sculptor, architect and landscape gardener. He was paricularly successful as an architect, but was criticized by Hogarth.

LOUTHERBOURGH, Philip James, R.A. (1740-1812). Painter, particularly of landscapes, battle scenes and marine subjects. He was born in Germany as Philippe Jacques de Louterbourg. He assisted Garrick as a designer of scenery and costumes.

MACARTNEY, George, lst Earl Macartney (1737-1806). Diplomat and colonial governor. He was Ambassador Extraordinary to Pekin, 1792-4.

POPE, Alexander (c. 1641-1717). Father of Alexander Pope, the poet. He was a Roman Catholic linendraper in London.

RICHMOND, Sir William Blake (1842-1921). Artist. He carried out mosaic work in the choir of St Paul's Cathedral. He mainly painted subjects from classical mythology.

ROSE, Dr William (1775-1843). Poet, and M.P. for the Chiltern Hundreds in 1800. His publications include rhymed translations from the *Amadis* of Herberay des Essarts, 1803.

SHARP, William (1744-1824). Engraver who had businesses in Bartholomew Lane, Vauxhall and Chiswick. He made plates after Reynolds, Guido and West. He was a friend of Thomas Paine and Horne Tooke.

THORNHILL, Sir James (1675-1734). Painter. He decorated St Paul's and Greenwich Hospital. His daughter, Jane, married Hogarth.

VILLIERS, Barbara, Countess of Castlemaine and Duchess of Cleveland (1641-1709). London beauty and mistress of Charles II, who acknowledged paternity of at least five of her children. John Churchill perhaps fathered another of her children. She was notorious for her amorous adventures.

WHISTLER, James Abott McNeill (1834-1903). American-born Impressionist painter and etcher. He was educated at the Military Academy in West Point. In 1878 he brought a libel action against Ruskin for condemning his picture *Nocturne in Black and Gold,* and was awarded a farthing's damages. Among his best-known works are *Portrait of my Mother* and *Westminster Bridge.*

FINSBURY

Clerkenwell Green

ST JAMES'S CHURCH

Underground: Farringdon

Buses: 170, 243

The church is on the site of the Benedictine nunnery of St Mary's, founded in the twelfth century. At the Dissolution of the Monasteries, the buildings were allowed to fall into ruin, but the parishioners bought the church. It was demolished in 1788 and replaced by another, built by James Carr. Among those buried here are two sons of Izaak Walton.

BELL, John (d. 1556). Bishop of Worcester in 1537. He was one of Henry VIII's chaplains and was consulted by him at the time of his divorce from Catherine of Aragon.

BURNET, Gilbert (1643-1717). Bishop of Salisbury and historian of his own times. He was very much anti-Catholic and reproved Charles II for dissolute living. He gave counsel to William and

Mary, and preached at their coronation. He preached in London churches and was chaplain of the Rolls Chapel. He was exiled three times for refusing the covenant.

CAVE, Edward (1691-1754). Printer. He was denounced in Parliament for publishing George II's answer to an address before it had been reported from the Chair. He also invented a spinning machine and published the *Gentleman's Magazine*. A friend of Samuel Johnson.

ELIZABETH, Countess of Exeter (d. 1653). Wife of Edward Cecil, grandson of Lord Burghley.

PERKINS, Richard and SUMNER, John (dates unknown). Famous actors before the Restoration.

WALTON—Two sons of Izaak Walton, both named Izaak. They died in 1650 and 1651, respectively.

WEEVER, John (1576-1632). Poet and antiquary. He published works on Shakespeare, Spenser and Ben Jonson. Also *Ancient Funeral Monuments,* 1631, a useful guide, as many were later destroyed.

St James's Church

WESTON, Prior (d. 1640). Last Prior of the Hospital of St John of Jerusalem.

FINSBURY

Clerkenwell Road ST JOHN'S CHURCH *(St John's Square)*

Underground: Farringdon Buses: 170, 243

There is an area marked on the cobbles of St John's Square indicating the former site of the round nave of the church of the Knights Hospitaller of St John of Jerusalem. Below is a fine twelfth-century crypt, all that is left of the magnificent priory. There is a small churchyard. An eighteenth-century brick building is all that remains above ground. This and the site belong to the Order of St John of Jerusalem. The little churchyard at the back of the church contains the graves of John Wilkes BOOTH (d. 1836) and other relatives of the assassin of President Lincoln.

FINSBURY

Pentonville Road

ST JAMES'S CHURCH

Underground: King's Cross

Buses: 8, 30, 73, 214

The church was built by Aaron Hunt in 1787, from subscriptions, and was used as a dissenting chapel. In 1791 it was consecrated and made into a Chapel of Ease to Clerkenwell Parish Church, becoming a parish church in 1854. The famous clown, Grimaldi, is among those buried here.

BONINGTON, Richard Parkes (1801-28). Painter. He studied water-colour painting at the Louvre and under Baron Gros. He also painted in oils, and produced very mature work for such a young painter. He died whilst on a visit to England.

GRIMALDI, Joseph (1779-1837). Actor and pantomime player. He appeared on the London stage at a very early age, dancing at Sadler's Wells and later at Drury Lane Theatre. His greatest success was as a clown in *Mother Goose* at Covent Garden.

STORER, Henry Sargant (1795-1837). Engraver and draughtsman who exhibited at the Royal Academy. He worked on many topographical subjects with his father, James Sargant STORER (1771-1853), an engraver, who is also buried here.

FINSBURY

Old Street

ST LUKE'S CHURCH

Underground: Old Street

Buses: 5, 55

This was a new parish in 1732 and it is not certain who the architect was—possibly George Dance the Elder. Part of the churchyard is now a garden.

ALLEN, Thomas (1803-33). Topographer who also illustrated volumes on London and several counties.

CASLON, William, the Elder 1692- 1766). Typefounder. He was born in Worcestershire where he was an engraver on metal. He started a shop and type-foundry in 1716.

FINSBURY

Charterhouse Square

SCHOOL CHAPEL

Underground: Barbican

A Carthusian priory was founded here in the fourteenth century, and in this area were buried 50 000 victims of the Black Death (1348-57). The school chapel was built not, as was thought, on the site of the old monastery, but on the chapterhouse area of the monastery. It was built by a rich benefactor, Thomas Sutton, circa 1611. In 1872 the Charterhouse School moved to Godalming in Surrey, and what was left of Charterhouse has been bought by St Bartholomew's Hospital.

FENNAR, Captain George (d. *circa* 1617). Buccaneer. He fought against five Portuguese ships for two days, and commanded the largest private galleon against the Armada. It is said that it was his ship which brought news of the

School Chapel, Charterhouse

approach of the Armada, although (according to John Smith) this act is also attributed to another privateer called Fleming.

PEPUSCH, John Christopher (1667-1752). Musical composer and organist at Charterhouse. He was born in Berlin and came to London in 1688 where he became famous as a teacher of the science of harmony.

RAINE, Matthew, D.D., F.R.S. (1760-1811). Headmaster at Charterhouse, 1791-1811.

SUTTON, Thomas (1532-1611). Founder of Charterhouse School and a hospital for Poor Brethren. A keen business man who had plans for exploiting the coalfields of Durham, he was estimated the richest commoner in England. His bowels are buried at Hackney.

FULHAM

Fulham High Street

Underground: Putney Bridge

ALL SAINTS

Buses: 22, 30, 74

Only the tower is left of the old church, which was built in the fifteenth century. The present building was completed in 1881. The first burials recorded in the large graveyard were in 1376. Several Bishops of London were buried here.

COMPTON, Henry (1632-1713). Bishop of London. Before this he was Bishop of Oxford and Dean of the Chapel Royal. He was a supporter of William of Orange, and crowned William and Mary in 1680. All his income was spent on charities.

GIBSON, Edmund (1669-1748). Bishop of London, 1720-48, and chaplain to Archbishop Tenison. Previously Bishop of Lincoln.

HAYTER, Thomas (1702-62). Bishop of Norwich and London. Preceptor to the Prince of Wales. He supported the Jews' Naturalisation Bill of 1753, and was made a Privy Councillor in 1761.

HOOK, Theodore Edward (1788-1841). Novelist, wit and friend of the Prince of Wales. He was educated at Harrow, and as a boy wrote scripts for his father's comic operas. He spent some time in Mauritius as an accountant general, but was dismissed for inefficiency, imprisoned, 1823-25, and had his property taken away from him. He published many novels and other works, including *Exchange no Robbery* (a farce), and edited *John Bull*.

MORDAUNT, John, 1st Baron Mordaunt of Reigate (1627-75). He planned an insurrection in Sussex, was arrested and imprisoned in the Tower, 1658, acquitted and raised to the peerage. He became

Constable of Windsor Castle in 1660. (Fine effigy by John Bushnell)

ROBINSON, John (1650-1723). Bishop of London. Chaplain to the English Embassy and Swedish Court, 1680. Later he became Dean of Windsor and Lord Privy Seal, 1711.

SHERLOCK, Thomas (1678-1761). Bishop of London. He was at Eton with Walpole and was later Master of St Catherine's Hall, Cambridge, then Vice-chancellor. He had a reputation as a fine preacher.

TERRICK, Richard (1710-77). Bishop of Peterborough and London. He was a Fellow of Clare College, Cambridge, and Preacher at the Rolls Chapel, 1736-57. He was Chaplain to George II and became a Privy Councillor in 1764.

ZOUCHE, Richard (1590-1661). A great authority on civil law. He published a book covering the whole field of law and examining in detail all its various departments. Judge of the High Court of the Admiralty, 1641.

HACKNEY

Lower Clapton Road   ST JOHN'S PARISH CHURCH

Buses: 22, 30, 38

A huge church which stands near the tower of an earlier one, St Augustine. The church probably changed its name because the Knights Hospitaller had buildings here. There i large churchyard.

CAREW, Sir Alexander (1609-44). M.P. for Cornwall and Governor for Parliament of St Nicholas's Island in Plymouth Harbour. He was arrested on suspicion of betraying his charge, found guilty and executed on Tower Hill.

DEFOE, Daniel (d. 1724). Infant son of the writer.

NEWCOME, Richard (d. 1769). Bishop of St Asaph.

PERCY, Sir Henry Algernon, 6th Earl of Northumberland (c. 1502-37). Warden of the eastern and western marches in 1527. He arrested Wolsey in 1530. He was accused of being the lover of Anne Boleyr but this charge was not proved.

ROWE or ROE, Owen (c. 1593-1661). Haberdasher of London. He was a membe of the court which tried Charles I, and signed his death warrant. He was convicte as a regicide in 1660, and died in the

Tower of London. He also took part in the foundation of the colonies of Massachusetts and the Bermudas.

VERE, Edward de (1550-1604). 17th Earl of Oxford and a poet. He was an important figure at Elizabeth I's Court, 1564-82, but fell out of favour because of his violent temper. He sat as one of the judges of Mary, Queen of Scots, 1586.

HAMMERSMITH

Queen Caroline Street

Underground: Hammersmith

ST PAUL'S CHURCH

The early church was built in 1626, later enlarged and restored in 1864 and rebuilt in 1882.

CRISP, Sir Nicholas (c. 1599-1666). A Royalist to whom Charles I gave the rights for trading with Guinea. He was M.P. for Winchelsea, but expelled from Parliament for collecting duties on merchandise without a Parliamentary grant. He helped Charles I to raise an army in 1643. He later fled to France, 1645, but returned at the Restoration. (Buried at the foot of the church-tower)

MORLAND, Sir Samuel (1625-95). Diplomat, inventor and mathematician. Inventor of a pump to raise water to the top of Windsor Castle. He suggested the use of high pressure steam in the propulsion of vessels and also invented a calculating machine.

MURPHY, Arthur (1727-1805). Dramatist, and editor of Fielding's works. He was refused entry to the Middle Temple because he was an actor, but was admitted to Lincoln's Inn. A friend of Samuel Johnson, he wrote a book on the latter's life, and another on Garrick.

SHEFFIELD, Edmund, 1st Earl of Mulgrave (c. 1564-1646). Commander of a squadron against the Spanish Armada.

WORLIDGE, Thomas (1700-66). Painter and etcher who worked in the style of Rembrandt.

HAMPSTEAD

Church Row

ST JOHN'S CHURCH, HAMPSTEAD PARISH CHURCH

Underground: Hampstead

The church was rebuilt in 1747 and an extension to the churchyard opened in 1844. Among the famous people buried here are John Constable, Norman Shaw, George Du Maurier, and, in recent years, Anton Walbrook, the actor, and Kay Kendall, the actress.

AIKIN, Lucy (1781-1864). Authoress. She compiled her historical memoirs of the Courts of Elizabeth I, James I and Charles I.

ASKEW, Anthony (1722-74). Classical scholar, and collector of books. Also a physician.

BAILLIE, Joanna (1762-1851). Scottish dramatist and poetess. Kemble and Mrs Siddons acted in her plays, the most successful of which was *The Family Legend.* Her *Fugitive Verses* was published in 1790.

CARTER, John (1784-1817). Architect. Draughtsman to the *Builder's Magazine,* 1774-86 and the Society of Antiquaries. He published many books of views of buildings in England (1780-1814).

CHARLES, Elizabeth (1828-96). Authoress whose writings consist mainly of tales and sketches of Christian life in different lands and ages. Her work attracted the attention of Tennyson.

CONSTABLE, John (1776-1837). Famous landscape painter. Although he exhibited his first landscapes at the Royal Academy in 1802, he was not really recognized in England, and made his living as a portrait painter. He made a great impression at the French *Salon* of 1824. Among his best-known works are *The Hay Wain* and *Salisbury Cathedral.* His wife Maria (*née* Bicknell) (1786-1828) is also buried here.

CORT, Henry (1740-1800). Ironmaster and inventor of the purifying process of iron by puddling. He was ruined in 1789 by the prosecution of his partner, Adam Jellicoe, for embezzlement of Naval funds.

HARRISON, John (1693-1776). Famous horologist and inventor of the gridiron pendulum, etc. His tomb in the churchyard was reconstructed by the Clockmakers' Company.

HONEY, Laura (*c.* 1816-43). Actress and singer. She had a great success as Psyche in *Cupid* and played at the Adelphi Theatre.

INGLETON, Charles (1763-1826). Tenor vocalist. He appeared at Covent Garden in the *The Beggar's Opera* and Haydn's *The Creation,* amongst other productions.

LESSINGHAM, Jane (d. 1783). An actress in the Covent Garden Company.

MACARDELL, James (*c.* 1729-65). Mezzotint engraver. He engraved many plates after Reynolds and Hudson.

MACKINTOSH, Sir James (1765-1832). Philosopher, historian and barrister. He also studied medicine at Edinburgh. He was the author of many books on philosophy, and of a *History of England.*

POPPLE, William (1701-64). Dramatist, though of rather mediocre talent. From 1745 he was Governor of the Bermudas.

RITCHIE, Lady Anne Isabella (1837-1919). One of Thackeray's daughters, and editor of his works.

SHAW, Richard Norman (1831-1912). Architect. His were the first ashes to be placed here. He trained as a Gothic architect and designed many country houses, also New Scotland Yard (Embankment) in 1891.

WEDGEWOOD, Hensleigh (1803-91). Philologist, and also a police magistrate. He published many books, including a *Dictionary of English Etymology,* 1857.

WEST or JENNY DIVER (d. 1783). A pickpocket.

EXTENSION

BESANT, Sir Walter (1836-1901). Novelist. His novels are not masterpieces, but are a very satisfactory combination of romance and realistic detail. He helped to found the Society of Authors and was an authority on the history of London.

DU MAURIER, George Louis Palmella (1834-96). Novelist and artist in black and white. He studied chemistry at University College, London and then art under Gleyre in Paris. He joined the staff of *Punch* as successor to John Leech and illustrated for the *Cornhill Magazine,* 1863-83. His famous novel *Trilby* was published in 1894. (Ashes deposited here)

GAITSKELL, Hugh Todd Naylor (1906-63). Chancellor of the Exchequer, 1950-51, and Leader of the Labour Party, 1955-63.

HARE, Sir John (1844-1921). Actor. His original name was John Fairs. He helped to develop modern English acting and was also theatre manager of the Garrick, 1889-95.

Kay Kendall

KENDALL, Kay (Harrison) (1927-59). Actress. She was especially talented at light comedy and appeared in several films of this type. One of them, *Genevieve,* made her a star. She was the wife of Rex Harrison, the actor, and died of leukaemia.

KNOX, Edmund George Valpy (1881-1971). His pseudonym was Evoe. He was a poet, author and satirist and he was the editor of *Punch,* 1932-49.

TREE, Sir Herbert Beerbohm (1857-1917). Actor. Son of an Anglo-German businessman and half-brother of Max Beerbohm. He took the name 'Tree' from the second part of his name, Beerbohm, which translates as 'peartree'. His first great success was in *The Private Secretary* in 1878. Regarded as a most versatile actor, he also appeared in several stage adaptations of Dickens's novels, and the plays of Ibsen, Wilde and Shakespeare. He was the last of the traditional actor-managers.

WALBROOK, Anton (1900-67). Actor. He was born in Vienna, as A. A. W. Wohlbrück. His first appearance on the London stage was in *Design for Living* at the Haymarket Theatre in 1939, and his notable films include *Sixty Glorious Years, Dangerous Moonlight* and *Gaslight.* (Ashes deposited here)

HOLBORN

St Giles High Street   ST-GILES-IN-THE-FIELDS

Underground: Tottenham Court Road   Buses: 8, 25

A hospital for lepers was founded on this site by Matilda, Queen of Henry I, in 1101. Its chapel was probably used as a church for the parish. At the Dissolution of the Monasteries, the old church was pulled down and a new one built. This in turn was pulled down in the seventeenth century, and the present one erected. Andrew Marvell is buried in the church.

ANNA MARIA, Countess of Shrewsbury (d. 1702). She disguised herself in the costume of a page, and held the horse of her lover, George Villiers, Duke of Buckingham, while he killed her husband, Charles Talbot, Earl of Shrewsbury, in a duel in 1668.

CHAPMAN, George (*c.* 1559-1634). Poet. Very little is known about his education. He completed Marlowe's *Hero and Leander* in 1598 and contributed to plays by Ben Jonson. His most famous works were rhyming-verse translations of Homer. He was imprisoned, probably for satirizing James I and his followers. His collected works were published in 1873-75

HANSARD, Luke (1752-1828). Printer. He was Printer to the House of Commons, printing the House of Commons journals. His two sons carried on this business.

L'ESTRANGE, Sir Roger (1616-1704). Tory writer. He wrote pamphlets in favour of the monarchy, and tried to show that the Presbyterians were responsible for the wars and for Charles II's death. At one stage he made plans for a Royalist uprising in Kent and had to escape to Holland.

MARVELL, Andrew, the Younger (1621-78). Poet and satirist. He was Milton's colleague in the Latin Secretaryship for Foreign Tongues in 1657. He wrote several poems in honour of the Protector, including *Horatian Ode upon Cromwell's Return from Ireland.* He strongly opposed the Government of Charles II.

MOHUN, Michael (*c.* 1620-84). Actor. He continued his acting career after service in the Royalist Army, and joined Killigrew's Company. He performed at the Cockpit Theatre.

PENDEREL, Richard (d. 1672). Staffordshire yeoman and Royalist. With his four brothers he helped in the escape of Charles II after the Battle of Worcester, and was rewarded and pensioned at the Restoration. (Table-tomb in the eastern part of the churchyard)

SHIRLEY, James (1596-1666). Dramatic poet, and master of St Albans Grammar School. He produced masques and plays, the most important being *The Cardinal, The Gamester* and *The Lady of Pleasure.* He was disparaged by Dryden, but his work was revived by Charles Lamb.

SHIRLEY, William (*fl.* 1739-80). Dramatist. His *Edward the Black Prince* was played by Garrick and Barry at Drury Lane in 1750. However, he later attacked Garrick in his writings.

HOLBORN

Tottenham Court Road

Underground: Goodge Street

WHITEFIELD'S TABERNACLE

Buses: 14, 24, 29, 73, 176

A chapel was built here for Whitefield in 1756, but a new one was erected in 1903. It was destroyed by one of the last rockets to fall on London at the end of the Second World War. A new chapel has now been built. Whitefield's has been Congregational for over a hundred years.

BACON, John, R.A. (1740-99). Sculptor whose works include Pitt's monument in Westminster Abbey and Dr Johnson's in St Paul's Cathedral. He received the first gold medal for sculpture in 1769.

TOPLADY, Augustus Montague (1740-78). Divine. He was converted to Wesleyanism in 1756, but not long after changed to extreme Calvinism. He then began a vendetta against Wesley, charging him with unfairness and clandestine printing. He published *Rock of Ages* in 1775. Died of consumption.

WHITEFIELD, Elizabeth James *née* Burnell (*c.* 1718-68). Wife of George Whitefield, leader of the Calvinistic Methodists and founder of tabernacles in London, Bristol and America.

KENSINGTON

Brompton Road   HOLY TRINITY CHURCH
Underground: South Kensington   Buses: 14, 30, 74

This church stands at the back of Brompton Oratory. The churchyard is now a small, pleasant garden, and the first burial here took place in 1829.

CORPE, John (d. 1829). His was the first interment in this churchyard, and the occasion of Letitia E. Landon's poem *The First Grave*. (In the south-west corner)

FARREN, Harriet Elizabeth (*fl.* 1813-57). Actress. Her first stage appearance in

London was as Desdemona. (Buried in central path)

REEVE, John (1799-1838). Actor and comedian. He appeared at Drury Lane as a mimic, and then at several other London theatres. He was often drunk and could not learn his parts, but was a great favourite with the public.

KENSINGTON

Kensington High Street   ST MARY ABBOT'S
Underground: High Street, Kensington   Buses: 27, 52, 73

So called because the church belonged to the Abbey of Abingdon in the Middle Ages. The old church was pulled down in the seventeenth century and replaced by another, which was in turn replaced by the present church, designed by George Gilbert Scott. There is a small churchyard.

ELPHINSTON, James (1721-1809). Educationalist and translator of Martial. After working as a private tutor, he established a school at Brompton and later in Kensington. He also translated several works from French (not very well). In 1778-82 he published a translation of Martial, against the advice of his friend Johnson, which was very much criticized. The rest of his life was devoted to evolving a system of phonetical spelling.

INCHBALD, Elizabeth (1753-1821). Dramatist, novelist and actress. She was self-educated and was an actress until 1789—with no great success. She then wrote about sixteen plays, most of which are translations. Her best-known work is a novel—*A Simple Story*—which was a great success and may, to a certain extent, have inspired *Jane Eyre*. She was a close

friend of Sarah Siddons and of John Kemble, and is said to have been a great beauty—her portrait is in the Garrick Club.

JORTIN, John (1698-1770). Vicar of Kensington and author of the *Life of Erasmus*. Before becoming Vicar of Kensington, he was Rector of St Dunstan's-in-the-East. His *Life of Erasmus* is a respected piece of work, but has long since been superseded. There is a portrait of Jortin at Jesus College, Cambridge.

MADAN, Rev. Martin (1726-90). Author. He led quite a gay life until he was converted to Methodism after hearing Wesley preach. Then he took orders and was appointed Chaplain to Lock Hospital. From 1750 to 1780 he also itinerated and preached at Bristol, Brighton—etc. In 1780 he published *Thelyphthora*, in which he advocated polygamy as being in accordance with Christianity, if properly understood. This raised such a storm of protest that he resigned his chaplaincy and retired to Epsom. He was a first cousin to Cowper.

LAMBETH

ST MARY'S CHURCH *(By Lambeth Palace)*

Buses: 3, 159

The church has very early foundations, but although the tower is fourteenth-century, the rest of the present church was built in 1852. The churchyard shares a wall with Lambeth Palace. Lambeth was for many years a seat of Bishops, and there are five Archbishops buried in the church.

BANCROFT, Richard (1544-1610). Archbishop of Canterbury. He was Treasurer of St Paul's in 1590, chaplain to Archbishop Whitgift in 1592, and Bishop of London in 1597. He worked against the Puritans. (Buried in church)

BARKER, Robert (1739-1806). Said to be the inventor of the panorama. He worked as a portrait painter, but while painting outside one day, he realized that if he painted on a cylindrical surface, he could present the whole of the scene around him. (Buried in church)

BLIGH, William (1754-1817). Captain of the *Bounty,* afterwards Vice-admiral of the Blue, 1814. He accompanied Captain Cook on his second voyage round the world, 1772-4. His overbearing conduct was one of the causes of the mutiny on the *Bounty*, when Fletcher Christian and the mutineers cast him adrift in an open boat with eighteen of his men. He later distinguished himself in the mutiny at the Nore, 1797. (Monument)

COOKE, Thomas (1703-56). Translator of Hesiod, and commonly called 'Hesiod Cooke'. He was a Whig journalist who attacked Pope and Swift anonymously. He published poems, translated many Greek classics and edited Virgil.

CORNWALLIS, Frederick (1713-83). Dean of St Paul's and Archbishop of Canterbury, 1768. He died at Lambeth Palace and was buried in a vault under the communion table.

DOLLOND, Peter (1730-1820). Optician. He opened his first shop in Strand, and was later joined in the firm by his father and uncle. They worked on the refractory telescope and discovered how to make achromatic lenses.

FORMAN, Simon (1552-1611). Astrologer. He claimed to have miraculous powers and practised as a quack doctor in London, where he had a great following among the Court ladies. In 1568 he began to practise necromancy. He was regarded as disreputable and an associate of his was convicted of the poisoning of Sir Thomas Overbury in 1613.

HUTTON, Matthew (1693-1758). Bishop of Bangor Archbishop of York, 1747-57 and Archbishop of Canterbury for one year only (1757). (In church)

MOORE, Edward (1712-57). Author and dramatist. He wrote several comedies, some of which were produced at Drury Lane. His *Dramatic Works* were published in London in 1788. He was buried in the graveyard without a stone to mark the spot.

NASMYTH, Patrick (1787-1831). A painter, who studied the Dutch landscape painters. He caught a chill while sketching trees on the Thames, and died propped up in bed watching a thunderstorm.

SECKER, Thomas (1693-1768).
Archbishop of Canterbury for ten years.
The son of pious dissenting parents, he
was sent, at the expense of Dr Isaac
Watts, to study divinity. He is buried in
a covered passage leading from Lambeth
Palace to the north door of Lambeth
Church. (No monument)

SOWERBY, James de Carle (1787-1871).
Naturalist and artist, noted for his
fossil drawings. The Natural History
Museum, Kensington has many of his
plates and descriptions. He resided at the
Royal Botanic Society's gardens in
Regent's Park for thirty years.

TENISON, Thomas (1636-1715).
Archbishop of Canterbury. He was Vicar
of St Andrews the Great, Holborn, at the
time of the Plague of 1665 and later
of St Martin-in-the-Fields. His most
important work as an Archbishop was for
the Society for the Propagation of the
Gospel. He preached the sermon at Nell
Gwyn's funeral.

THIRLEBY, Thomas (c. 1506-70).

Bishop of Westminster. He was one of
the convocation which recognized Henry
VIII as supreme head of the English
Church, and he later signed the decree
annulling Henry VIII's marriage to Anne
of Cleves, 1540. He died as a prisoner in
Lambeth Palace during Queen Elizabeth
I's reign.

TRADESCANT, John (d. circa 1637).
Collector and horticulturist. He
travelled to Russia in 1618 and made the
first collection of plants and berries of
that country. He had a physic garden and
museum at South Lambeth. (Also buried
here are his son (1608-62) and grandson
(1635-52), both also called John
Tradescant.)

TUNSTALL or TONSTALL, Cuthbert
(1474-1559). Bishop of Durham and
London at the time of Mary I and Master
of the Rolls. He was tried and deprived
of his bishopric by an act of parliament
in 1552, but was restored to the
bishopric of Durham in 1554, only to
lose it again for refusing the oath of
supremacy under Elizabeth.

MARYLEBONE

St John's Wood High Street
ST JOHN'S WOOD CHAPEL now called ST JOHN'S WOOD CHURCH

Underground: St John's Wood   Buses: 2, 2a, 2b, 13, 26, 113

*The chapel was built in 1814 as a Chapel of Ease to St Marylebone Parish Church. The
architect was Thomas Hardwick. It stands in a small but wide graveyard, now used as a
park.*

BROTHERS, Richard (1757-1824).
Midshipman and master's mate. He was
called a crazy mystic and supposed
prophet because he declared himself a
descendant of David. In 1795 he was
arrested on a charge of treasonable prac-
tices and put in an asylum at Islington. He
was released in 1806 and published *A
Revealed Knowledge of the Prophecies
and Times.*

FARQUHAR, John (1751-1826).
Munitions-millionaire and landowner of
Fonthill Abbey.

GODLEY, Samuel (1781-1832). Private
in the 2nd regiment of Life Guards. His
daring and courage displayed when
charging the French cuirassiers at the
Battle of Waterloo brought him much
acclaim. (Inscription on grave)

JACKSON, John (1778-1831). Portrait painter, of humble origins. He studied at the Royal Academy with Haydon and Wilkie.

SOUTHCOTT, Joanna (1750-1814). Prophetess and fanatic. A Devonshire farmer's daughter, she worked as a domestic servant for many years. In 1792, she began to write prophecies and broke with her Methodist teaching. After publishing her strange dreams, she began to make converts, and in 1802 she declared that she was going to bring into the world a spiritual man—Shiloh. She died of a brain disease. (Buried under the name of Goddard)

TERRY, Daniel (*c.* 1780-1829). Actor and playwright. He appeared at Drury Lane and at Covent Garden in works by Shakespeare and Sheridan. A friend of Sir Walter Scott.

TREDGOLD, Thomas (1788-1829). Engineer and author of *The Steam Engine,* 1827, and *Elementary Principles of Carpentry,* 1820.

TURNERELLI, Peter (1774-1839). Sculptor who exhibited at the Royal Academy and was tutor to the royal family. He executed many busts, including one of Wellington, and memorials—e.g., that of Robert Burns at Dumfries.

MARYLEBONE

ST MARYLEBONE OLD PARISH CHURCH
(At the top of Marylebone High Street)

Underground: Baker Street

Buses: 30, 176

The burial ground is in the High Street and belonged to the Old Parish Church which was painted by Hogarth in The Rake's Marriage *and which was demolished in 1949. The present church is in Marylebone Road. Among those buried in the High Street are George Stubbs and Charles Wesley.*

ABBADIE, Jacques (*c.* 1654-1727). Religious writer and Dean of Killaloe. After the Battle of the Boyne he came to London where he became minister of the French Church in the Savoy. He published many religious works.

BOWER, Archibald (1686-1766). Historian. After studying divinity at Rome he came to England, where he conformed to the English Church. He was proved guilty of being a secret member of the Catholic Church, and was later re-admitted as a Jesuit. Author of the *History of the Popes* (7 vols), 1748-66.

CRAMER, Wilhelm or William (*c.* 1745-99). Violinist. He appeared in many musical performances and was a member of the Royal Society of Musicians in 1777.

FERGUSON, James (1710-76). Astronomer. At the age of nine he was considered a genius in mechanics. He constructed a terrestrial globe and invented a tide dial, 1754, and a universal dialling cylinder, 1767. He also painted portraits.

FIGG, James (d. 1734). Pugilist and teacher of boxing and swordsmanship at his own academy in Marylebone. There he exhibited bear and tiger-baiting.

HOLCROFT, Thomas (1745-1809). Dramatist and author. Besides writing and producing many plays he also acted in musical plays and comic operas.

HOYLE, Edmond (1672-1769). Writer on card games. He taught whist in Queen Square, London, and published a

Short Treatise on Whist in 1742. Later editions of the book also included backgammon, quadrille and chess.

RAMSAY, Allan (1713-84). Painter. After studying in London and Europe he became a portrait painter in Edinburgh, but later came to London again, where he was portrait painter to George III in 1767. He was considered by Walpole to be a better painter of women than Reynolds.

RYSBRACK, John Michael (c. 1693-1770). Sculptor. He studied in Antwerp and came to England in 1720. Many of his portrait busts and groups can be seen in London—several of them are in Westminster Abbey.

SERRES, Dominic (1722-93). Marine painter. He served as a master on trading ships to Havana, but was captured by a British ship and brought to England in 1758. He settled here and became marine painter to George III.

STUBBS, George (1724-1806). Animal painter. After studying anatomy in York and travelling in Italy, he settled in London in 1756 and became well-known for his studies of horses. He was probably the first painter to master the anatomy of the horse. He did portraits for Lord Grosvenor and the Duke of Richmond.

VANDERBANK, John (c. 1694-1739). A portrait painter whose subjects included Isaac Newton. He also illustrated *Don Quixote*.

WANLEY, Humphrey (1672-1726). Bibliophile and antiquary. Assistant in the Bodleian Library, Oxford, and librarian to the Earls of Oxford.

WESLEY, Charles (1707-88). Poet and younger brother of John Wesley. He was ordained in 1735, and wrote over six thousand hymns including *Jesu, Lover of My Soul*. He is buried here at his own request. (Monument)

WHEATLEY, Francis (1747-1801). Landscape painter. He worked in both water-colour and oils, and also painted portraits and a popular series, *The Cries of London*.

PADDINGTON GREEN

ST MARY'S CHURCH

Underground: Edgeware Road   Buses: 6, 8, 16

The present church, which is the oldest church in Paddington, was built in 1789 on the site of an earlier one. John Bushnell, the sculptor, and Matthew Dubourg, the violinist, were buried in the old church. The burial ground is now a pleasant park.

BANKS, Thomas (1735-1805). Sculptor. He studied under Peter Scheemakers and exhibited at the Royal Academy, 1780-1805. He was arrested for high treason at the same time as his friend, Horne Tooke. There are works by him in Westminster Abbey, and St Paul's.

BARRET, George, the Elder (c. 1728-84). Painter. He studied in Dublin and taught drawing, but later achieved success in England as a landscape painter.

BRYAN, Michael (1757-1821). Author of the *Biographical . . . Dictionary of Painters and Engravers*, 1813-16.

BUSHNELL, John (c. 1606-1701). Sculptor. He studied in France and Italy. Among his works are many sculptures for buildings in London including Temple Bar. He died insane.

COLLINS, William, R.A. (1788-1847). Popular painter of portraits and figures.

DUBOURG, Matthew (1703-67). Violinist. He played at Covent Garden in Handel's oratorio concerts, and also gave concerts at Lincoln's Inn Fields.

GEDDES, Alexander (1737-1802). Writer and critic of the historical books and publisher of the historical books of the Old Testament. His critical remarks on the Hebrew scriptures brought protests and caused his suspension from ecclesiastical functions.

HALL, John (1739-97). Line engraver and historical engraver to George III in 1785. He engraved Benjamin West's works.

HAYDON, Benjamin Robert (1786-1846). Historical painter. His stormy personality caused some upsets with his fellow painters. He was imprisoned for debt several times, and committed suicide after his exhibition failed and his designs for the House of Commons were rejected. Among his pupils were the Landseers, Eastlake and Bewick. Wordsworth and Keats addressed sonnets to him. (Buried just outside of hallowed ground.)

NOLLEKENS, Joseph Francis (1702-48). 'Old Nollekens'. Painter of conver- sation pieces. He studied under Watteau and Panini.

NOLLEKENS, Joseph (1737-1823). Sculptor. The son of Joseph Francis Nollekens. He was trained by Peter Scheemakers and worked for the Royal Academy, 1771-1816. His monuments were much admired. He became partially paralysed and gradually fell into a state of imbecility.

SCHIAVONETTI, Luigi (1765-1810). Line engraver, born in Italy, who came to England in 1790, where he became the assistant of Francesco Bartolozzi.

SIDDONS, Mrs Sarah (1755-1831). Actress. The daughter of Roger Kemble. She started acting at a very early age and became a most versatile actress, well- known for her Shakespearean roles. She acted at Drury Lane, Covent Garden, etc., and also gave private readings at Windsor Castle. Her statue is beside the church and another, by Chantrey, is in Westminster Abbey.

VIVARES, François (1709-80). An engraver who worked mainly from landscape painters. He was French, but settled in London in 1727.

ST PANCRAS

Hampstead Road

ST JAMES'S CHURCH

Underground: Euston

Buses: 24, 29, 134

In 1788 this site was made into an established burial ground for St James's Church, Piccadilly. It was closed for burials in 1853 and is now a private garden, although part of it is covered by Euston Station. The church was built in 1791 by Thomas Hardwick the Younger.

CHRISTIE, James, the Elder (1730-1803). Founder of the famous London auction rooms. Father of James (1773-1831).

DICKSON, Dr William (1745-1804). Irish Bishop. He was educated at Eton and Hertford College, Oxford, and ordained Bishop of Down and Connor in 1783. He was a friend of Charles James Fox.

GARDNER, Alan, 1st Baron Gardner (1742-1809). Admiral. He was with Rodney in the *Duke* at the sea battles in the West Indies in 1782, and was made a baronet for his services during Howe's victory of 1794 (against the French). A friend of Nelson and M.P. for Plymouth.

GORDON, Lord George (1751-93). Agitator and Protestant champion. He presented a petition which led to the Popery riots of 1780, was charged with treason, and acquitted, 1781. He was later converted to the Jewish faith. He died in Newgate, having been imprisoned since 1788 for libelling the British Government and Queen Marie Antoinette of France.

HOPPNER, John (1758-1810). Portrait painter, born in London of German parents. He exhibited at the Royal Academy in 1780 and 1809, his finest portraits being *Lady Cullin*

(Eardley) Smith and Children and *Mrs Lascelles.* He was a chorister in the Chapel Royal.

MORLAND, George (1763-1804). Painter. He first exhibited at the Royal Academy at the age of ten. His pictures, which show the influence of Flemish and Dutch painters, reflect lowly life in rural England. Morland was arrested for debt in 1799 and released in 1802, but died in a sponging house. He wrote his own epitaph–'Here lies a drunken dog'.

SCHNEBBELIE, Jacob (1760-92). Topographical artist who made many drawings of London. He became drawing master and draughtsman to the Society of Antiquaries, and was also a confectioner, living at Canterbury and Hammersmith.

ST PANCRAS

St Pancras Road
ST PANCRAS OLD CHURCH—ST PANCRAS GARDENS

Underground: King's Cross   Buses: 214

This was the first church to be erected in the county of Middlesex, circa 1180. The present church was built in 1380, but much restoration work was done in 1848 and 1888. It was the last parish church where Roman Catholic rites were carried out. It was in this churchyard, now a garden, that Dickens set the mock funeral and attempt at bodysnatching in a Tale of Two Cities. *The thief Jonathan Wild's body was disinterred from this church and his skeleton placed in the Royal College of Surgeons on public exhibition. With the building of the railway from St Pancras Station, part of the burial ground was ploughed up and the headstones placed in the churchyard. Among those buried here are John Flaxman, the sculptor, Sir John Soane, the architect, and Johann Christian Bach.*

BACH, Johann Christian (1735-82). German composer. He was born in Leipzig, the eleventh son of Johann Sebastian Bach. After his appointment as organist at Milan Cathedral he was appointed composer to the King's Theatre, London. He was made music master to Queen Charlotte in 1763.

BLEWITT, Jonathan (*c.* 1780-1853). An opera composer, who also wrote panto-mime music for most of the London theatres.

BLOUNT, Martha (1690-1762) and Teresa, her sister. (d. 1759). Friends of Alexander Pope. He dedicated to Martha his *Epistle on Women,* and at his death left considerable property to her.

COLLIER, Rev. Jeremy (1650-1726). A non-juror who published numerous pamphlets against William III. He was outlawed in 1696, although not arrested, and published a *Short View of the Immorality and Profaneness of the English State* in 1698, and also an *Ecclesiastical*

History of Great Britain. He was ordained as a non-juring Bishop in 1713.

COOPER, Samuel (1609-72). Miniature painter whose subjects included Cromwell and Milton.

DE CORT, Henry Francis (1742-1810). Landscape painter. He was born in Antwerp where he was secretary to the Antwerp Academy in 1788. He exhibited at the Royal Academy from 1790.

D'EON DE BEAUMONT, Charles Geneviève Louis Auguste André Timothée, Chevalier (1728-1810). Secret agent of the King of France at St Petersburg in 1755, and Secretary to the French Embassy there, 1757-60. Later Minister Plenipotentiary in London, during which time he secretly corresponded with the King of France on a projected invasion of England. He was generally suspected of being a woman, as he wore women's clothing, but on his death was found to be a man.

EDWARDS, Edward (1738-1806). The author of *Anecdotes of Painters* and Professor of Perspective at the Royal Academy in 1788. He published fifty-two etchings in 1792.

FLAXMAN, John, R.A. (1755-1826). Sculptor. He gained a considerable reputation for his drawings, both in England and in Italy, where he spent several years, and was the first Professor of Sculpture at the Royal Academy. Amongst his most famous works are the statues of Burns and Kemble at Westminster Abbey. The British Museum has a collection of his drawings.

HIGGONS, Bevil (1670-1735). Author of an attack on Bishop Gilbert Burnet's *History of his own Time.*

LEONI, Giacoma (1686-1746). Architect. He was a Venetian but settled in England at the beginning of the eighteenth century and designed various country seats. He made plates for the

English edition of Palladio's *Architecture,* 1715.

MALCOLM, James Peller, F.S.A. (1767-1815). Topographer and engraver. He was born in Philadelphia but came to London where he studied at the Royal Academy. He was the author of *Londinium Redivivum* (a history and description of London).

MAZZINGHI, Tommaso (d. *circa* 1775). A Corsican wine merchant who settled in London and became violinist at Marylebone Gardens. The father of Count Joseph Mazzinghi, the composer.

MILLS, John (d. 1811). The last survivor of those who came out of the Black Hole of Calcutta in West Bengal in 1756.

PASQUALINO, Peter (d. 1766). Famous 'cello player who brought the 'cello into fashion in England.

PAXTON, Stephen (1735-87). Violoncellist and composer.

RACKET, Henry (d. 1775), and Robert (d. 1774). Nephews of Alexander Pope.

SCHEEMAKERS, Thomas (1740-1808). Sculptor, and son of Peter Scheemakers. He exhibited at the Royal Academy, 1765-1804.

Sir John Soane

SOANE, Sir John, R.A. (1753-1837).
The architect who rebuilt the Bank of
England. He was Professor of Architecture
at the Royal Academy in 1806, and was
the founder of the Soane Museum of
paintings and works of art.

THEOBALD, Lewis (1688-1744).
Editor of Shakespeare, 1734, and hero of
the early editions of the *Dunciad*. In
1727 he produced *The Double Falsehood*,
a tragedy, as a work of Shakespeare, but
it was probably from his own pen. He
published many translations from Greek
writers.

WALKER, John (1732-1807).
Lexicographer. He started his career as an
actor, 1758-68, but later became a teacher
and lecturer. He published several text

books on elocution and English grammar,
and in 1791 published his *Pronouncing
Dictionary*. The stone was preserved by
Baroness Burdett-Coutts.

WEBBE, Samuel, the elder (1740-1816).
Composer of vocal music, particularly
part-songs and church music. He came
from a poor family and was apprenticed
to a cabinet-maker for seven years as a
child.

WOODHEAD, Abraham (1609-78).
Champion of the Roman Catholic
faith, who firmly opposed the Puritan
leanings of the Government. He was
tutor to George Villiers, second Duke of
Buckingham, and the author of controversial and religious works.

SHOREDITCH

ST LEONARD'S CHURCH (PARISH CHURCH)

Underground: Shoreditch   Buses: 6, 22

*Early documents show that there was a church here in the thirteenth century. This was
pulled down and replaced by the present church in 1899.*

BURBAGE, Richard (c. 1567-1619).
Actor. He lived in Shoreditch and
acted at the theatre there as a child. He
had shares in Blackfriars Theatre and also
in the Globe Theatre. He appeared in
productions of plays by Shakespeare
and Jonson.

COWLEY, Richard (d. 1619). One of
the original actors in Shakespeare's
plays.

GREENE, Fortunatus (d. 1593). Poet
and player. Illegitimate son of the more
famous Robert Greene, poet and playwright.

LILLO, George (1693-1739). A
dramatist who helped to popularize

the domestic drama of England. His
most famous work is *The London
Merchant, or The History of George
Barnwell*, 1731, a tragedy.

MANNERS, Frances, *née* Sidney,
Countess of Rutland (1583-1612). Only
child of Sir Philip Sidney.

SLY, William (d. 1608). One of the
original performers of Shakespeare's
plays. Sly's date of birth is unknown.
He lived in Horse-shoe Alley in
Bankside from 1593 to 1605.

SOMERS, William (d. 1560). Court
jester to Henry VIII.

SPENCER, Gabriel (d. 1598). A player
who was killed in a duel by Ben Jonson.

TARLTON, Richard (d. 1588). Actor, of humble origin. Queen Elizabeth I was attracted by him and made him one of her twelve players, and Shakespeare is thought to have identified his Yorick with him. He invented a doggerel verse called 'Tarletonizing'. Died in poverty.

WARD, Ned (1667-1731). Humorist who kept a tavern in London. He published a great number of coarse poems satirizing the Whigs, the Low-Church party and life in London. His work *The London Spy* was published in parts, 1698-1709.

SOUTHWARK

Borough High Street
ST GEORGE THE MARTYR'S CHURCH

Underground: Borough   Buses: 501, 513

The present church was built in 1736, but the first recorded date for a church on this s
is 1122. For many years prisoners who died in the Marshalsea Prison were buried here.

BONNER or BONER, Edmund (*c.* 1500-69). A notorious Bishop of London, and the last of the Ruthvens. He died in the Marshalsea Prison, where he had been sent for refusing to take the Oath of Supremacy.

COCKER, Edward (1631-75). Arithmetician and book collector. *Cocker's Arithmetick* went into more than a hundred editions.

HAWKINS, John (d. 1695). The editor of Cocker's works.

RUSHWORTH, John (*c.* 1612-90). Historian, barrister and secretary to

Cromwell. He accompanied Fairfax on campaigns in 1645, and was M.P. for Berwick five times. He spent the last six years of his life in prison.

TATE, Nahum (1652-1715). Dramatist and poet. He was appointed Poet Laureate in 1692. The Christmas carol *While Shepherds Watched* is attributed to him. He was satirized in *The Dunciad*.

WOOLSTON, Thomas (1670-1733). He wrote controversial religious tracts and published his ideas on the founding of a new sect. He was imprisoned, for his *Discourses* on Christ's miracles, in 1729.

SOUTHWARK

Borough High Street   SOUTHWARK CATHEDRAL

Underground: London Bridge   Buses: 501, 513

Formerly St Saviour's, it is known to have been built on a Roman site. It was originally
the church of the nunnery of St Mary Overie. In the ninth century this was changed in
an Augustinian priory by St Swithin, Bishop of Winchester. Although part of the
church was used for the parish in the thirteenth century, it was not used as a parish
church until 1540, when the name was changed to St Saviour's. It attained cathedral
status in 1904. Among those buried in the Cathedral are John Gower, the poet, and
many actors from the theatres of Bankside.

ANDREWES, Lancelot (1555-1626). Bishop of Winchester and previously Bishop of Ely. He was well-known for his

devotional writings. One of those involved in the publication of the Authorized Version of the Bible.

AUSTIN, William (1587-1634). Barrister of Lincoln's Inn. Author of *Godly Meditations*. He resided in Southwark and was a friend of Edward Alleyn, the founder of Dulwich College. (Monument)

AUSTIN, William (*fl.* 1662). Barrister of Gray's Inn and also a poet and classical scholar. He was the son of the above, and is buried near the monument to his father.

DYER, Sir Edward (d. 1607). Poet and courtier, knighted by Elizabeth I in 1596. One of his best-known poems, *My mind to me a kingdom is,* was set to music by William Byrd. Most of his fame was gained in the last quarter of the sixteenth century. A friend of Sir Philip Sidney.

FLETCHER, John (1579-1625). Dramatist. He lived on Bankside, near the Globe, with the poet, Francis Beaumont, together with whom he wrote plays. Fletcher was probably the less talented of the two, but he excelled at brilliant dialogue and lively repartee. His plays include *Women Pleased* and *Wildgoose Chase,* and many were performed at Drury Lane. He died of the plague and is thought to be buried in the same grave as Philip Massinger (see below), with whom he formed a partnership.

FLETCHER, Lawrence (d. 1608). Actor and co-lessee of the Globe Theatre, and one of the leading shareholders in the Globe and Blackfriars Theatres.

GOWER, John (*c.* 1325-1408). Poet, described by Caxton as 'a squyer borne in

Walys in the time of Kyng Richard the second' (*sic*). His chief work, *Confessio Amantis,* was written at the request of Richard II. In other works he takes the seven deadly sins as his subject and also denounces the clergy. Gower was acquainted with Chaucer, but it is thought that they were not the best of friends and used to have personal disagreements. In their day they were regarded as being of equal poetic stature, but time has declared Chaucer the greater. (Miniature in the British Museum)

MASSINGER, Philip (1583-1639). Dramatist. He wrote some fifteen tragedies and comedies, many of which are now lost, but which included *The Bondman, A New Way to Pay Old Debts,* etc. He associated with John Fletcher (see above) in writing plays for the Cockpit Theatre. He died suddenly at his house on Bankside, near the Globe Theatre, and was buried in the middle of this churchyard.

NEWLAND, Abraham (1730-1807). For many years he was chief cashier of the Bank of England. The banknotes bearing his well-known signature were known as 'Abraham Newlands'. There is a portrait of him, by Romney, in the Bank of England.

SHAKESPEARE, Edmund (*c.* 1580-1607). Actor and youngest brother of William Shakespeare.

TREHEARNE, John (d. 1618). A gentleman porter to James I.

STEPNEY   Stepney High Street   ST DUNSTAN'S CHURCH

Underground: Stepney Green

Bus: 25

The manor of Stepney was granted to the Bishops of London in A.D. 604. A small church was built on the site by Dunstan in the tenth century, and an ancient Saxon rood, which can be seen over the communion table today, probably belonged to this earlier church. The present church was restored in 1847. Among those buried here are Richard Pace, friend of Erasmus, and Dean Colet.

COLET, Sir Henry (d. 1505). Father of Dean Colet (see below). He was Lord Mayor of London in 1486 and 1495.

COLET, John (*c.* 1467-1519). He was vicar of this church, Dean of St Paul's 1504-19, and the founder of St Paul's

School. He travelled in Italy and knew Erasmus, to whom he paid an annuity.

CRAB, Roger (c. 1621-80). One of the most eccentric characters of the seventeenth century. He was a strict vegetarian, living on roots and herbs and drinking only water. He served in the Parliamentary Army, but was later imprisoned for being a quack doctor. He is said to have foretold the Restoration and the accession of William of Orange.

ENTICK, Rev. John (c. 1703-73). Schoolmaster and author of histories, English and Latin dictionaries and spelling books.

KENTON, Benjamin (1719-1800). Wealthy vintner and philanthropist. He was educated at a Whitechapel charity school, but made a great deal of money by keeping a tavern. In 1776 he was made a master of the Vintners' Company. He was benefactor of Sir John Cass's School and of St Bartholomew's Hospital.

LEAKE, Sir John (1656-1720). Admiral of the Fleet and a Lord of the Admiralty in 1709. With his fleet he destroyed scores of French ships and, as Governor in 1702, seized French settlements in Newfoundland. M.P. for Rochester, 1708-14.

MEAD, Matthew (c. 1630-99). Famous nonconformist and minister at several London churches. He was the guardian of James Pierce, the Exeter heretic, in 1680. He was suspected of complicity in the Rye House plot, but was discharged. In 1690 he assisted in the amalgamation of the Presbyterian and Congregational bodies.

PACE, Richard (c. 1482-1536). Diplomatist. He was a friend of Erasmus, was vicar of this church, 1519-27, and also Dean of St Paul's Cathedral.

SPERT, Sir Thomas (d. 1541). Founder and first Master of the Corporation of Trinity House.

STRYPE or van STRIJP, John (d. 1648). A rich merchant and father of John Strype, the biographer and historian. He came from Brabant and set up as a merchant and silk-throwster in an area, in Petticoat Lane, which was later known as 'Strype's Yard'. He became a Freeman of the City of London.

STEPNEY

Tower

ST PETER AD VINCULA

Underground: Tower Hill

This is a parish church which was used mainly for the garrison and prisoners in the Tower. A chapel possibly existed from Henry I's reign (c. 1100), and was rebuilt and restored several times. The church holds poignant memories as it was situated near the scaffold and was the burial place of many who were beheaded. Within the chancel are the graves of fifteen of noble blood; all but two of these died on the block. Howes wrote—'here lyeth before the high altar in St Peter's church, two Dukes, betweene two Queenes, to wit, the Duke of Somerset and the Duke of Northumberland between Queene Anne and Queene Catherine, all four beheaded.' The last burial in the chapel was Charles Wyndham, Keeper of the Regalia, in 1872.

ARUNDELL, Sir Thomas, of Lanherne (d. 1552). Gentleman of the Privy Chamber to Wolsey and Commissioner for the Suppression of the Monasteries in 1535. He was imprisoned in the Tower for alleged implication in the Cornish rising of 1550, and was executed for his activity in Somerset's 'conspiracy'.

St Peter Ad Vincula. Execution spot in foreground

BOLEYN, Anne (1507-36). Second Queen of Henry VIII. He married her secretly in 1533, after taking proceedings against his wife, Catherine of Aragon, with a view to a divorce. Anne was later condemned for high treason; Mark Smeaton, a musician, was arrested for criminal intercourse with the Queen and condemned for high treason, along with William Brereton, groom of the Queen's Bedchamber. Anne was executed on 19th May 1536, two days after she had been made to watch the executions of her supposed lovers—five in all, including her brother, Viscount Rochford (see above). Only the Queen and Viscount Rochford were buried in the chapel. The executioner was brought over from Calais.

BOLEYN, George, Viscount Rochford (d. 1536). Brother of Anne Boleyn. In 1530 he was knighted and made Viscount Rochford, and in 1534 made Warden of the Cinque Ports. He was condemned for incest and high treason, and executed.

BOYD, William, 4th Earl of Kilmarnock (1704-46). General and Privy Councillor to Prince Charles, the Young Pretender. He fought at Falkirk with Lord Balmerino in 1746, was captured at the Battle of Culloden, and executed on Tower Hill.

CROMWELL, Thomas, Earl of Essex (c. 1485-1540). Statesman. One of the commissioners appointed by Cardinal Wolsey to enquire into the state of the monasteries in 1525. It was he who suggested to Henry VIII the policy of making himself head of the Church of England and thus to obtain his divorce from Catherine of Aragon, and who later conveyed Anne Boleyn to the Tower in 1536. He was accused of treason by the Duke of Norfolk and executed.

DEVEREUX, Robert, 2nd Earl of Essex (1566-1601). Favourite of Queen Elizabeth I, who created him a knight for his bravery. He was later proclaimed a traitor for plotting to secure the dismissal of Elizabeth's counsellors and attempting to raise the citizens of London. It is said that Elizabeth was willing to pardon him if he asked her forgiveness. When he was beheaded his executioner is said to have narrowly missed death at the hands of the crowd. He wrote many sonnets and was the patron of Spenser and Jonson.

DUDLEY, John, Duke of Northumberland (c. 1502-53). Governor of Boulogne 1544-6, created Earl of Warwick and High Chamberlain of England in 1547. He married his son to Lady Jane Grey in 1553, and was executed for actively resisting the succession of Mary to the throne. He avowed himself a Roman Catholic on the scaffold. Whilst in prison, he amused himself by carving a puzzle-picture, the Dudley coat-of-arms, on one of the walls.

ELIOT, Sir John (1592-1632). Patriot and Member of Parliament for Cornwall in 1628. He was imprisoned several times for his defence of parliamentary liberties, and died in the Tower.

ELPHINSTONE, Arthur, 6th Lord Balmerino (1688-1746). Jacobite. He escaped to the Continent, where he remained for several years, but was taken prisoner after the Battle of Culloden and sent to the Tower. At his execution he appeared in full regimental robes and a wig which he then replaced with a cap of Scottish plaid, saying that he died a Scotsman.

FANE or VANE, Sir Ralph (d. 1552). He was hanged at the Tower for plotting to murder the Duke of Northumberland in 1551.

FISHER, John (1459-1535). Bishop of Rochester and opponent of Henry VIII's divorce from Catherine of Aragon. He was imprisoned in the Tower in 1534 for refusing to swear to the Act of Succession, and was sentenced to die a traitor's death of hanging, disembowelling and quartering, but the writ was changed at the last minute to beheading. He was responsible for Erasmus's coming to Cambridge and wrote treatises against Luther.

FITZGERALD, Gerald, 9th Earl of Kildare (1487-1534). He was imprisoned in the Tower for treason in connecting himself by marriage with the Irish enemy. He was released, but later imprisoned again and died in the Tower.

FRASER, Simon, Lord Lovat (c. 1667-1747). Jacobite intriguer. He was arrested for high treason in the 1745 rebellion and beheaded on Tower Hill. Apparently the scaffold collapsed before his execution and he is said to have remarked—'The mo mischief, the better sport'.

GREY, Henry, Duke of Suffolk (d. 1554) Father of Lady Jane Grey. He was pardoned by Mary for his involvement in the plan to put Jane Grey on the throne, but later joined the rising against the Spanish Marriage and was beheaded for treason. Before his arrest he hid with his brother in his gamekeeper's cottage, but the gamekeeper betrayed him and he was found hiding in a hollow tree.

(Head in St Botolph's Church, Aldgate)

GREY, Lady Jane (1537-54). Queen of England. She was very beautiful and talented, speaking several languages. Her reign, at the age of sixteen, lasted only nine days and she was beheaded on Towe Hill. At her execution she did not know how to place her head on the block, but tied her handkerchief over her eyes, refusing the headsman's aid.

GREY, Thomas, 15th and last Baron Grey of Wilton (d. 1614). He fought against the Spanish Armada. He was invol ved in the Bye plot against James I, but reprieved on the scaffold in 1603 and remained in the Tower until his death.

HOLLAND, John, Duke of Exeter and Earl of Huntingdon (1395-1447). Admira of England and Constable of the Tower. His remains were brought here from Regent's Park in 1951.

HOWARD, Catherine (d. 1542). Fifth Queen of Henry VIII, who married her secretly. She had clandestine relations with her cousin, Thomas Culpepper. Her maidservants supplied evidence of her affairs with her music master, Henry Mannock, and Francis Dereham, a retainer of the Duchess of Norfolk, before her marriage, but evidence of adultery after marriage was sought in vain. She was beheaded at the Tower on 13th February 1542.

HOWARD, Philip, 1st Earl of Arundel (1557-1595). Eldest son of Thomas Howard, fourth Duke of Norfolk. He had been converted to Roman Catholicism in 1584. He was imprisoned for life for attempting to escape from England, and in 1589 he was condemned to death on a charge of saying mass for the success of the Spanish Armada. However, he was not executed, but remained in the Tower for life.

HOWARD, Thomas, 4th Duke of Norfolk (1536-72). Son of Henry Howard, Earl of Surrey. He succeeded his grandfather as Duke and Earl Marshal in 1554, and helped in the building of Magdalene College, Cambridge. He was arrested for his involvement in Roberto Ridolfi's plot to overthrow Elizabeth's government, and was executed for treason. However, he denied having been a papist.

MOORE, Sir Jonas (1617-79). Mathematician. He was tutor to the Duke of York in 1647, surveyor of the Fen drainage system in 1644 and Surveyor-general to the Ordnance, 1683. He was also the author of A New System of the Mathematicks.

MORE, Sir Thomas (1478-1535). Lord Chancellor of England and a distinguished man of letters. He was accused of infringing the Act of Supremacy, found guilty and sentenced to be hanged at Tyburn, but this was commuted to decapitation on Tower Hill. Catholic Europe was shocked by his execution. More was a great patron of the arts; his Latin verse and prose are regarded in Catholic circles as among the glories of literature. One of his most famous works was his Utopia,

1515-16. He was canonised with John Fisher in 1935.

MURRAY, William, Marquis of Tullibardine (d. 1746). A Jacobite who was taken prisoner after the Battle of Culloden in 1746, and died in the Tower.

OKEY, John (d. 1662). Colonel of dragoons at the Battle of Naseby in 1645. He signed Charles I's death warrant in 1649, and was later arrested for opposition to Cromwell. After escaping to Germany, he was arrested in Delft and later executed at the Tower.

OVERBURY, Sir Thomas (1581-1613). Poet. After refusing diplomatic employment, he was sent to the Tower in 1613. While there, he was slowly poisoned with white arsenic by agents of Frances Howard, Countess of Essex, whose marriage to Robert Carr, Earl of Somerset, he had opposed. Four of the agents were later hanged for this, although Carr and his wife were pardoned.

PERROT, Sir John (c. 1527-92). He was lord deputy of Ireland and thought to be an illegitimate son of Henry VIII. He made many errors of government in Ireland and returned in disgrace in 1588. He was committed to the Tower, found guilty of high treason, and died there.

POLE, Margaret, Countess of Salisbury (1473-1541). Daughter of George Plantagenet, Duke of Clarence. She was appointed governess to Princess Mary by Henry VIII. On his marriage to Anne Boleyn, she refused to give up the young princess's jewels and lost favour. After Anne's fall she returned to Court but was compromised by her son Reginald Pole's work De Unitate Ecclesiastica, for which Henry determined to destroy the Pole family and had Margaret executed. It is said that at her execution she refused to lay her head on the block, saying 'This is for traitors and I am none', and ran round the block defying the headsman with shrieks, so that 'he was compelled to fetch her off slovenly'.

Also buried here are her two grandsons: ARTHUR (1531- *c.* 70) and EDMOND (1541- *c.* 70), both found guilty of treason but too young to be executed. They were imprisoned in the Beauchamp Tower, Edmond in the upper and Arthur in the lower room. Both carved inscriptions on the walls, which can be still be seen. Her son, Henry, Lord Montague (*c.* 1492-1539) also died in the Tower, as well as another grandson also named Henry.

ROETTIERS or ROTIER, John (1631-1703). Medallist and official engraver to the Mint, where he made English and Scottish coins. He was also Engraver-general to the French Mint in 1703.

SCOTT, James, Duke of Monmouth and Buccleuch (1649-85). The illegitimate son of Charles II. He married Anne Scott and took the name of Scott in 1663. In 1670 he was Captain-general of Charles II's forces and served aginst the Dutch and the French. He joined in a plot to murder Charles and the Duke of York, though because he revealed the plot to Charles, was pardoned but banished from Court. On Charles' death, he claimed legitimate and legal right to the Crown as head of the Protestant forces. He was proclaimed king at Taunton, but defeated by Feversham and Churchill at Sedgemoor in 1685, captured and executed at the Tower.

SEYMOUR, Edward (*c.*1506-1552). 1st Earl of Hertford and Duke of Somerset. Lord Protector. He was the brother of Jane Seymour. He held an important position in Henry VIII's household and brought Anne of Cleves to London in 1539. His radical religious reforms produced much unrest; he was arrested on a charge of plotting to murder the Earl of Warwick, condemned for felony and beheaded on Tower Hill.

SEYMOUR, Thomas, Baron Seymour of Sudeley (*c.*1508-49). Ambassador to the Regent of the Netherlands, and Admiral of the Fleet. He secretly married the Queen Dowager, Catherine Parr, in 1547, and after her death was interested in a marriage with Princess Elizabeth. He also sought to marry Lady Jane Grey to Edward VI. However, he was arrested and imprisoned in the Tower, found guilty of treason and executed.

WHITECHAPEL

Adler Street   CHURCHYARD OF ST MARY MATFELON

Underground: Whitechapel   Buses: 25

A Church has stood here since before 1300, the last one being destroyed in the Second World War.

BRANDON, Richard (d. 1649). Known as 'Young Gregory'. He was the executioner of Charles I. He was given £30 for this, all paid in half-crowns. He also executed the Earl of Holland and the Duke of Hamilton with the same axe he had used on the King. He was said to have prepared himself for his calling by decapitating cats and dogs.

PARKER, Richard (*c.* 1767-97). Mutineer who joined the navy to avoid a prison sentence for debt. He was chosen president by the mutineers at the Nore, 1797, and was hanged after the collapse of the mutiny.

CHURCHES & CHURCHYARDS OUTSIDE THE CITY OF LONDON

1. All Saints, Camberwell
2. All Saints, Fulham
3. Christ Church, Victoria Street
4. Grosvenor Chapel, Westminster
5. Holy Trinity, Brompton Road
6. St Anne's, Soho
7. St Clement Danes, Westminster
8. St Dunstan's, Stepney
9. St Giles, Camberwell
10. St Giles-in-the-Fields, Holborn
11. St George the Martyr, Southwark
12. St James's, Clerkenwell Green
13. St James's, Hampstead Road
14. St James's, Pentonville Road
15. St James's, Piccadilly
16. St John's, Clerkenwell Road
17. St John's, Hackney
18. St John's, Hampstead

19. St John's Wood Chapel
20. St Leonard's, Shoreditch
21. St Luke's, Old Street
22. St Margaret's, Parliament Square
23. St Martin-in-the-Fields
24. St Mary Abbot's, Kensington
25. St Marylebone
26. St Mary Matfelon, Whitechapel
27. St Mary's, Lambeth
28. St Mary's, Paddington Green
29. St Nicholas's, Chiswick Hall

30. St Pancras Old Church
31. St Paul's, Covent Garden
32. St Paul's, Hammersmith
33. St Peter Ad Vincula
34. Savoy Chapel, Westminster
35. School Chapel, Charterhouse Square
36. Southwark Cathedral
37. Westminster Abbey
38. Westminster Cathedral
39. Whitefield's Tabernacle

CEMETERIES AND BURIAL GROUNDS

A. Abney Park, Stoke Newington
B. Brompton, Kensington
C. Bunhill Fields and the John Wesley Chapel, Finsbury
D. Chelsea Hospital Burial Ground and the Moravian Burial Ground
E. Highgate
F. Jewish Burial Grounds

G. Kensal Green and St Mary's R.C.
H. Norwood
I. St George and St George the Martyr, Bloomsbury
J. St Martin's Gardens, Camden Town
K. The Gardens, Paddington Street
L. West Hampstead

FINSBURY

This was the principal burial place of the nonconformists from 1685 until 1854. The name is thought to be a corruption of 'bonehill'—the resting place for the bones disinterred from St Paul's by Edward Seymour, Duke of Somerset, in 1547.

BLAKE, William (1757-1827). Poet, and artist and mystic. He printed his own poems from etched copper plates and illustrated them by hand. Among his most famous poems and engravings are *Songs of Innocence and Experience,* 1789-94, *Inventions to the Book of Job,* 1820-6, and *Prophetic Books,* 1793-1804. He also wrote the well-known poem *Jerusalem,* which has since been set to music. His favourite saying, which he translated into his art, was, 'All things exist in the human imagination alone'. His wife, Catherine (1762-1831), is buried with him. (The memorial stone does not mark the actual site.)

BRADBURY, Thomas (1677-1759). Congregational minister and pastor of an independent congregation in New Street, Fetter Lane. He refused the bribe of a bishopric under Queen Anne. He published many religious and political works.

BUNYAN, John (1628-88). Author of *Pilgrim's Progress.* Born in Elstow, Bedford, he began in his father's trade of tinsmith. He was deeply moved by the death of a comrade in the Parliamentary Army who was shot while serving in his (Bunyan's) place. In 1661, he was arrested for preaching, and imprisoned. He continued to preach while in prison and resumed itinerant preaching on his release in 1672. His collected works were published in 1736. (Recumbent effigy on tomb.)

CROMWELL, Henry, Richard and William. Descendants, but not sons, of Oliver Cromwell.

DEFOE, Daniel (*c.* 1661-1731). Novelist, satirist and pamphleteer. He was a dissenter and an agent of both Godolphin and Harvey. He published over 250 works among which are *Robinson Crusoe,* 1719, *Journal of the Plague Year,* 1722, and *Moll Flanders,* 1722. He changed his name from Foe to Defoe in 1703.

DOOLITTLE, Thomas (*c.* 1632-1707). Pastor of St Alphege, London Wall. He opened a boarding school at Moorfields and also published theological treatises.

FAUNTLEROY, Henry (1785-1824). Banker and forger who was arrested for fraudulently selling stock in 1820, and for forging the trustees' signatures to a power of attorney. Executed, despite many petitions on his behalf.

FLEETWOOD, Charles (d. 1692). Parliamentarian General. He was wounded at the first battle of Newbury in 1643. He married Cromwell's eldest daughter, Bridget, and supported Richard Cromwell in opposition. At the Restoration he was prevented for life from holding office.

FOX, George (1624-91). Founder of the Society of Friends. The son of a Leicestershire weaver, he became an itinerant preacher and was imprisoned at Nottingham for brawling in church in 1649. He protested against the Presbyterian system, and recruited his friends from the lower middle-classes. He made missionary journeys to America and the West Indies. (Buried at Whitecross Street, Bunhill Row)

BUNHILL FIELDS (JOHN BUNYAN'S TOMB)

GOODWIN, Thomas, the Elder (1600-80). Independent divine. He attended Cromwell on his deathbed, and with John Owen drew up the amended Westminster confession. He was the founder of the City Temple.

HARDY, Thomas (1752-1832). Radical politician and bootmaker. He founded the London Corresponding Society to promote Parliamentary reform, 1792. In 1794 he was charged with high treason, but acquitted.

HART, Rev. Joseph (c. 1712-68). Independent preacher at Jewin Street Chapel, 1760-8, and author of many hymns.

KIPPIS, Andrew (1725-95). Nonconformist, biographer and divine. His chief literary work was the second edition of *Biographica Britannica.*

KNOLLYS, Hanserd (c. 1599-1691). Baptist divine. He became a separatist and renounced his orders in 1636. In 1645 he gathered his own church. He held offices under Cromwell, but fled to Germany at the Restoration. He later returned and was arrested under the Conventicle Act of 1670.

NASMITH, David (1799-1839). Originator of city and town missions and secretary to many charities in Glasgow. He also founded other charities in Ireland, the USA, France and London.

NEAL, Daniel (1678-1743). Historian. His *History of the Puritans* was published in four volumes and was translated into Dutch. He also published a *History of New England.*

OWEN, Dr John (1616-83). Dean and Vice-chancellor of Christ Church, Oxford. He accompanied Cromwell to Ireland and Scotland in 1650, as his Chaplain. After the Restoration he defended nonconformists and spoke against the Roman Catholic religion.

POWELL, Vavasor (1617-70). Nonconformist divine and itinerant evangelist in Wales *circa* 1639, who was the creator of a band of missionary preachers. He was arrested at the Restoration because of his refusal to abstain from preaching, and spent most of the rest of his life in prison.

PRICE, Richard (1723-91). Nonconformist minister and writer on economics, morals and politics. He was a friend of Benjamin Franklin and was invited by Congress to live in America.

QUARE, Daniel (1648-1724). Clockmaker. He worked in Exchange Alley and other parts of London. He invented repeater watches and made a clock for William III which needed winding only once a year. He was Master of the Clockmakers' Company in 1708 and he was subjected to persecution as a Quaker.

REES, Dr Abraham (1743-1825). A tutor in Hebrew and mathematics at Hackney College. He re-edited Ephraim Chambers's *Cyclopedia,* and then worked on *The New Cyclopedia* which appeared in forty-five volumes.

STOTHARD, Thomas (1755-1834). Painter and book illustrator. He designed the shield presented to Wellington and decorated Burghley House. He also executed illustrations for Milton, Spenser, Fielding, Sterne and Chaucer's *Canterbury Tales.*

TILLING, Thomas (d. 1760). Executed at Tyburn for the murder of his master.

WATTS, Isaac (1674-1748). Hymn writer. The son of a nonconformist schoolmaster, he composed 600 hymns, including *Behold the glories of the Lamb, Jesus shall reign where'er the sun* and *God our help in ages past.* He also published manuals on logic and the history of scripture.

WESLEY, Susannah, wife of Samuel (d. 1742). Mother of John and Charles, and also of seventeen other children.

WHITEHEAD, George (*c.* 1636-1723). A Quaker who was frequently imprisoned and severely persecuted for his views. He published controversial works dealing with his creed.

WILLIAMS, Daniel (*c.* 1643-1716). Nonconformist divine. The founder of the Williams Theological Library, which is housed in University Hall, Gordon Square, London. He refused to endorse James II's declaration as to liberty of conscience.

City Road

JOHN WESLEY CHAPEL

Underground: Old Street

Buses: 76

WESLEY, John (1703-1791). Leader of the Methodist and Evangelist movement. The fifteenth child of Samuel Wesley, rector of Epworth. He was educated at Oxford and much influenced by the writings of St Thomas à Kempis. Ordained in 1725, he became curate to his father. He gathered a group of young men round him at Oxford, who were interested in Methodism. In 1784, he unwillingly broke with the Anglican Church owing to the vast numbers joining the Methodists. He had great eloquence as a preacher. (His grave is in the centre of the small burial ground behind the chapel)

John Wesley   (Centre)

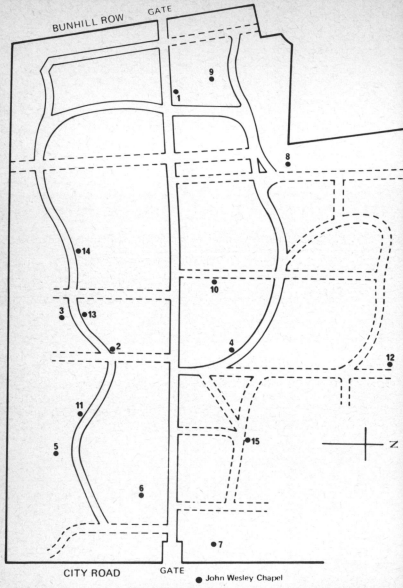

SKETCH PLAN OF BUNHILL FIELDS CEMETERY

BUNHILL ROW   GATE

8

9

1

14

10

3   13

2

4

11

5

12

6

15

7

CITY ROAD   GATE   ● John Wesley Chapel

z

1. BRADBURY Thomas
2. BUNYAN John
3. CROMWELL Family
4. DEFOE Daniel
5. FLEETWOOD Charles

6. GOODWIN Thomas, the Elder
7. HARDY Thomas
8. HART Rev. Joseph
9. KIPPIS Andrew
10. NEAL Daniel

11. OWEN Dr John
12. REES Dr Abraham
13. STOTHARD Thomas
14. WESLEY Susannah
15. WILLIAMS Daniel

HIGHGATE CEMETERY

The old cemetery was designed by Stephen Geary, who had a reputation as a gin palace architect. Like Kensal Green, Brompton and Nunhead, Highgate was opened to relieve the overcrowded burial grounds of central London. Besides fulfilling this function, it also became a favourite walk for Londoners and visitors. The cemetery covers an area of approximately thirty-eight acres. Today the old cemetery is closed because of vandalism. It is gradually becoming more and more overgrown and wild life is returning to it; at night one can often hear foxes as well as other animal and bird life. The new cemetery was opened only seventeen years after the old. Being a fashionable cemetery in Victorian times, there are a number of famous people buried here including the Rossettis, Michael Faraday and George Eliot.

à BECKETT, Gilbert Abbott (1811-56). Journalist and comic writer. He was the first editor of the *Figaro in London* and was on the original staff of *Punch*. He was also leader writer of *The Times* and the *Morning Herald* and a contributor to the *Illustrated London News*. He was a Metropolitan Police magistrate in 1849.

CHALON, Alfred Edward, R.A. (1780-1860). Artist and miniaturist. He was celebrated for his portraits of 'courtly and well-born ladies', and was the first to paint Queen Victoria after her accession to the throne.

CHALON, John James (1778-1854). Landscape and genre painter. His best-known works are *A view of Hastings* and *The Arrival of the Steam-Packet at Folkestone*. With his brother, Alfred Edward (see above) he founded an evening sketching-club which included Leslie and Clarkson Stanfield amongst its members.

COPLEY, John Singleton, the Elder (1737-1815). Portrait painter. He was born in Boston, Massachusetts, and had considerable success in America before going on a study-tour of Europe. When war broke out in America he settled with his family in London. As well as many fine portraits he painted works of a historical or imaginative nature. He was the father of Lord Lyndhurst (see below).

COPLEY, John Singleton, the Younger, Lord Lyndhurst (1772-1863). Lord Chancellor. Son of John Singleton Copley (see above). He was born in Boston, but brought to England in 1775. He became a barrister and in 1824-6, Attorney General. He conducted the prosecution of Queen Caroline before the House of Lords in 1820.

CRUFT, Charles (*c.* 1852-1938). Founder of the famous dog show. He worked for James Spratt, the dog-biscuit manufacturer, and became manager of the firm. He organized the first dog show in 1886.

DICKENS Family. Charles Dickens's parents, John Dickens (d. 1851) and Elizabeth Barrow (d. 1863), his wife, Catherine Hogarth (1815-79), and Dora Annie (1850-1) his ninth child. (Grave overgrown and difficult to find).

DRUCE, Thomas Charles (1793-1864). In 1896 Mrs Anna Maria Druce, the widow of T.C. Druce's son, Walter, claimed that Druce had in fact been William John Cavendish Bentinck-Scott (1800-79), fifth Duke of Portland, an eccentric recluse. Despite her constant appeals to have the vault opened, it was not until 1907, four years after she had been admitted to a mental home, that the vault was opened. In 1908 the last hearing on this strange case took place, and the body in the vault declared to be that of Thomas Charles Druce. Several people were consequently charged with perjury.

FARADAY, Michael (1791-1867). Chemist and philosopher. He began his career as a laboratory assistant in the Royal Institution, a post which he obtained through Sir Humphry Davy. In the next twenty years, he was responsible for many important discoveries—electro-magnetism, induction of electric currents, etc. He was made Fullerian Professor of the Royal Institution in 1833, and director in 1845 after his discovery of diamagnetism. He was very religious and a member of the Sandemanians.

HALL, Radclyffe (1886-1943). Writer. Her real name was Mabel Veronica Batten. In 1928 she wrote *The Well of Loneliness,* an intense novel, about the attachment between a young girl and an older woman, which was banned for some time in Britain. She was a member of the council of the Society for Psychical Research.

HOLL, Francis Montague (1845-88). Portrait painter. Known as Frank Hall, he exhibited at the Royal Academy from 1864. His sitters included the Duke of Cambridge and the future King Edward VII.

HUGHES, David Edward, F.R.S. (1830-1900). Inventor, electrician and Professor of Music. He was born in London, but educated in Kentucky, USA. He improved the type-printing telegraph and invented the microphone almost simultaneously with Lüdtge, 1878.

HULLMANDEL, Charles Joseph (1789-1850). Lithographer. In 1818 he issued his *Views of Italy,* drawn and lithographed by himself, and in 1824 his *Art of Drawing on Stone.*

LANDSEER, Thomas (1795-1880). Engraver and etcher, mainly of the works of his brother, Edwin Henry Landseer.

LILLYWHITE, Frederick William (1792-1854). English cricketer, known as the 'Nonpareil Bowler'. He was a bricklayer by trade, but later became a professional cricketer, playing his first match at Lord's in 1827. The monument shows his wicket being uprooted—'bowled out finally by death'.

MAURICE, John Frederick Denison (1805-1872). Divine and Professor of Moral Philosophy at Cambridge. He inaugurated the Working Men's College in Red Lion Square, London, and was chosen as its Principal. He strongly advised the abolition of university tests in 1853. He helped to found the Christian Socialist Movement.

ROBINSON, Henry Crabb (1775-1867). Diarist. He trained as an articled attorney and worked in a solicitor's office in London. He then travelled in Europe where he met Goethe and Schiller. In England he was acquainted with Coleridge, Lamb and Wordsworth. He was a founder of the Athenaeum Club. Thirty-five volumes of his *Diary* and his *Letters* were published posthumously.

ROSS, Sir William Charles (1794-1860). Miniature painter. He was admitted to the schools of the Royal Academy at the age of fourteen, and won many medals for his work. He later became assistant to the miniaturist Andrew Robertson, and then a successful miniaturist himself. His subjects included Queen Victoria and many members of the royal family. There is a portrait of him in the South Kensington Museum.

ROSSETTI Family
Gabriele Rossetti (1783-1834)—Italian poet and writer.
Christina Georgina Rossetti (1830-94)—Poet and daughter of Gabriele. Among her best known works is *Goblin Market,* 1862.
William Michael Rossetti (1829-1919) and his wife, Lucy Maddox Brown (1843-94).

Dante Gabriel Rossetti (1828-82). Poet and painter. He formed the Pre-raphaelite Brotherhood with Millais, Holman Hunt—etc. The death of his wife, Elizabeth Siddal, two years after their marriage, affected him so much that he enclosed his writings in her coffin. They were taken out and published seven years later.

SAYERS, Tom (1826-65). Pugilist who was beaten only once in his life, and that was after sixty-one rounds. His most famous fight was with John C. Heenan, and lasted two hours and six minutes. Towards the end of the fight, Sayers was in danger of being strangled as he was trapped in the ropes. These were cut and the fight declared a draw. Sayers retired after this with his record intact. His funeral was attended by some 10 000 people. (The dog on the monument is a replica of a favourite pet and is not buried in the grave)

Tom Sayers

TENNYSON, Frederick (1807-1898).
Poet. He was the elder brother of Alfred,
Lord Tennyson, who overshadowed him
as a poet.

TURNER, Charles, A.R.A. (1774-1857).
Engraver. He produced more than 600
plates, mainly in mezzotint but also in
aquatint. He engraved many of the
plates of J.M.W. Turner's *Liber Studiorum,*
and they later became close friends. He
was engraver to George III in 1812. The
British Museum possesses a complete
collection of Turner's work.

VANDENHOFF, John M. (1790-1861).
Actor of Dutch descent. He worked
mainly in the west of England.

WOOD, Ellen (1814-87). Novelist,
known as Mrs Henry Wood. She was
the author of *East Lynne,* which sold
over half a million copies within a few
months, and many other popular works.

WYMARK, Patrick Carl (1926-70). Actor.
His real name was A.K.A. Cheeseman and
he began his acting career in 1951. He
was a member of the Old Vic Company,
1951-3. He is best-known for his television role in *The Power Game.*

New Cemetery

HIGHGATE CEMETERY

BETTY, William Henry West (1791-1874).
Actor, known as the 'Young Roscius'.
He played Romeo and Hamlet at the age
of twelve, and appeared at Drury Lane and
Covent Garden. He retired in 1824.

CLIFFORD, William Kingdom (1845-
79). Mathematician, metaphysician, and
author of philosophical treatises. He was
an atheist. He published *Elements of
Dynamics,* 1879-87.

COOPER, Abraham, R.A. (1787-1868).
Artist who mainly painted battles and
horses—of which he had a great knowledge. As a boy he worked as an assistant
in Astley's Theatre.

DAUKES, Whitfield (1811-80). Architect.
Designer of the Agricultural College,
Cirencester, and Colney Hatch Lunatic
Asylum. (He is buried in the family
vault)

EGAN, Pierce, the elder (1772-1849).
Sports writer, author of *Boxiana or
Sketches of Modern Pugilism,* and *Sports
and Mirror of Life.* He also wrote a
series of sketches describing London
amusements in Regency times—*Life in
London*—which was very popular.

ELIOT, George (1819-80). Novelist. Her
real name was Mary Anne Evans but she
wrote only one book under this name—
a translation of Feuerbach's *Essence of
Christianity.* She formed a great attachment with George Henry Lewes, with
whom she lived until his death—his grave
is behind hers. Her works include
Middlemarch, Adam Bede and *The Mill
on the Floss.* She stopped writing when
Lewes died and later married John W.
Cross, a New York banker, in 1880.

FOYLE, William Alfred Westropp (1885-
1963) Founder of the famous bookshop
in Charing Cross Road. Also buried here
is his son, William Richard Foyle(1912-57).

FRIESE GREENE, William (1855-1921).
The first person to make a moving film
in celluloid. In the early 1900s he was
also experimenting with talking films,
colour and 3-D photography. On his
death he was found to be almost penni-
less.

GALSWORTHY, John (1867-1933).
Novelist and playwright, best-known for
his series of novels comprising *The
Forsyte Saga.* (Memorial—his ashes were
scattered on the Sussex Downs)

GARNETT, Dr Richard (1835-1906).
Keeper of printed books in the British
Museum and author of several poetic,
critical and biographical works.

GEARY, Stephen (1797-1854).
Architect of Highgate Cemetery, 1839.

HOLMAN, James (1786-1857). Traveller,
who, in spite of the fact that he was
blind, travelled alone all over Europe,
Siberia, Africa, America and Australia,
and wrote *Voyage round the World,
1827-32.*

HOLYOAKE, George Jacob (1817-1906).
Social reformer who aided the spread of
the co-operative movement. He was
imprisoned for atheism. He was a Chartist
in 1832, and an Owenite in 1838.
(Monument with his bust)

HONEY, George (1822-80). Actor and
singer. He appeared in opera and
played eccentric roles.

KNIGHT, Charles (1791-1873). Author
and publisher. He produced many cheap
books on general knowledge, including
the *Penny Magazine* and *Penny Cyclopedia.*

LEVI, Leone (1821-88). Jurist,
statistician and expert on commercial law.
He was born of Jewish parents in Ancona,
but settled in England. He wrote papers
on the wages and earnings of the working
classes, and was appointed to the new
Chair of Commerce at King's College,
London. He later published his lectures.

LEWES, George Henry (1817-78).
Writer and critic. In 1851 became
acquainted with George Eliot and lived
with her for the rest of his life. He wrote
novels, plays and also a *Life of Goethe,
1855.* (Grave behind George Eliot's)

MARX, Karl Heinrich (1818-83).
Professor of Philosophy and the founder
of modern socialism. He was born in
Trier, Prussia, of Jewish origin, and

George Holyoake

studied at Bonn and Berlin. After being
expelled to Paris, he moved to Brussels,
then back to Germany, and when he was
again ordered to leave, settled in London
for the rest of his life. He studied at the
British Museum and helped found the
International Working Men's Association
in London, 1864. The first volume of
his work *Das Kapital* appeared in 1867,
but he died before the last two volumes
were published. He had a life-long friendship with Engels, in collaboration with
whom he wrote the *Communist Manifesto*
1847. Also buried in his grave is his
daughter, ELEANOR (1855-98), who
took her own life at the age of forty-three
His monument was severely damaged by
a bomb in 1974.

MORTON, Andrew (1802-45). Portrait
painter. He exhibited his work at the
Royal Academy, but died on the eve of
his election to the Academy.

PHELPS, Samuel (1804-78). Actor. He appeared at the Haymarket and at Covent Garden with Macready, and is reputed to have been the first actor to make Shakespeare a profitable enterprise for nearly twenty years. He became a manager and produced many Shakespearean plays.

PLATT, Sir Thomas Joshua (c. 1790-1862). King's Counsellor in 1834 and Baron of the Exchequer, 1845-56.

ROSA, Carl August Nicholas (1843-89). Musician, originally called Rose. He formed the Carl Rosa Opera Company in London 1875. His son, who was killed at Ypres, is also buried here.

SOWERBY, George Brettingham, the elder (1788-1854). Artist and conchologist who published catalogues of shells.

SOWERBY, James De Carle (1787-1871). Naturalist and artist. Son of James Sowerby, the naturalist. He was Secretary of the Royal Botanic Society and Gardens, 1838.

SPENCER, Herbert (1820-1903). Philosopher. He put forward the theory of organic evolution seven years before Darwin's *Origin of Species* was published. He was the author of books on the encouragement of the natural development of children's intelligence, and the inventor of a mechanical invalid-bed. He also attempted to account systematically for all cosmic phenomena. His influence, in his day, was world-wide.

WATSON, Musgrave Lewthwaite (1804-47). Sculptor and painter. He worked in the studios of Sir Francis Chantrey and William Behnes, and sculpted the bas-relief *The Battle of St Vincent* on Nelson's column.

WATTS, Alaric Alexander (1797-1864). Poet and editor of the *Literary Souvenir* until its demise in 1838. He became bankrupt in 1850 and his last job was with the Inland Revenue.

WOMBWELL, George (1788-1850). Menagerie proprietor. He started as a London bootmaker. In 1804 he purchased two boa constrictors and by exhibiting them covered their cost in three weeks. He then proceeded to collect a travelling menagerie which became one of the best in England. His memorial stone has a lion on it.

WYATT, Mathew Cotes (1777-1862). Sculptor, son of James Wyatt, the architect. His equestrian statue of Wellington, which was placed on the Decimus Burton arch at Hyde Park Corner, caused a storm of protest and was later removed to Aldershot.

YATES, Edmund (1831-94). Novelist. He worked first in the Post Office where he was head of the missing-letter department. He later became drama critic of the *Daily News*. During this period he offended Thackeray by a personal attack on him and was expelled from the Garrick Club because of this. He later joined the staff of the *New York Herald*.

ST MICHAEL'S CHURCH CRYPT
(Adjoining cemetery)

COLERIDGE, Samuel Taylor (1772-1834). Poet, critic and philosopher. Born in Devon. He failed to gain a degree at Cambridge. He resided in Highgate for the last nineteen years of his life. Among his most famous works are *The Ancient Mariner, Kubla Khan* and *Biographia Literaria.* He was a close friend of Wordsworth with whom he collaborated in the *Lyrical Ballads* of 1798. He showed great promise which was not fulfilled, perhaps due to his addiction to opium. (In the crypt of St Michael's church adjoining the cemetery).

SKETCH PLAN OF HIGHGATE CEMETERY

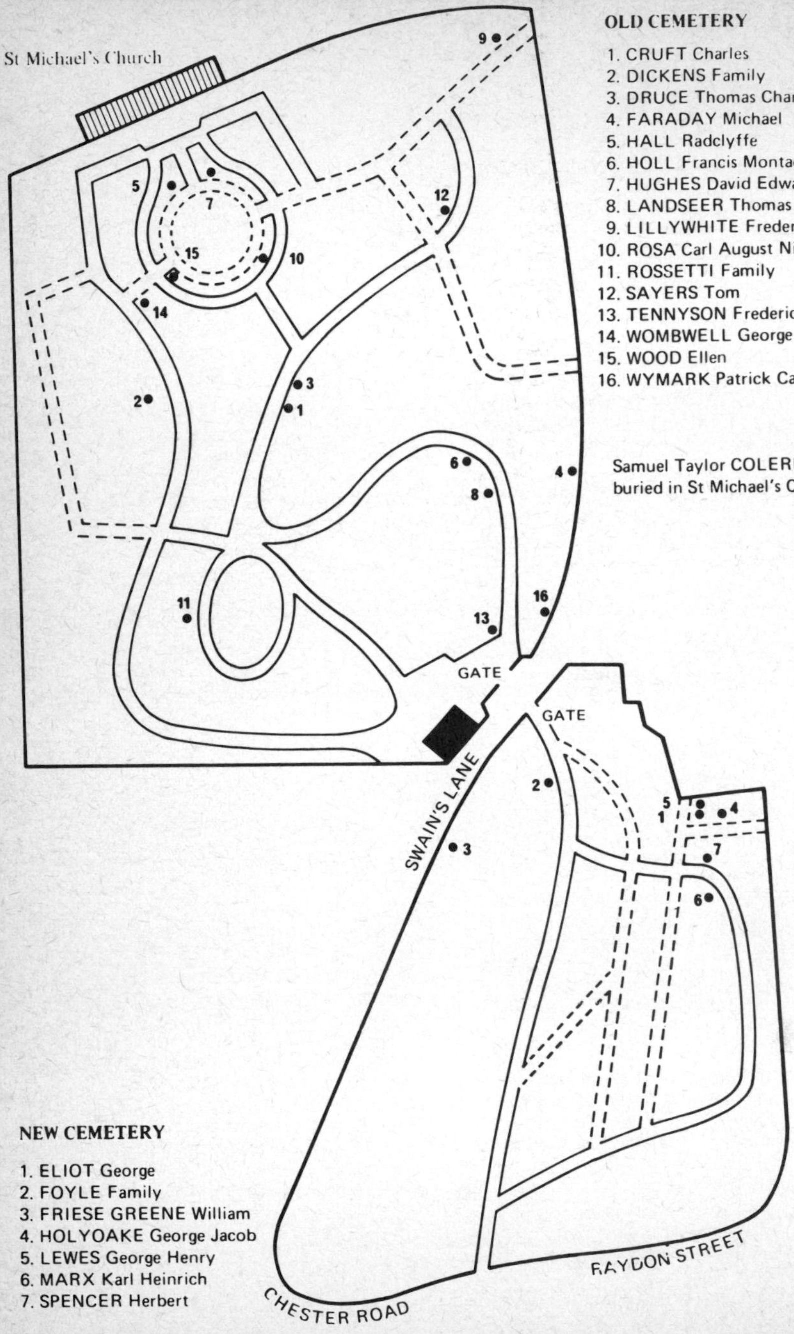

St Michael's Church
GATE
GATE
SWAIN'S LANE
RAYDON STREET
CHESTER ROAD

OLD CEMETERY

1. CRUFT Charles
2. DICKENS Family
3. DRUCE Thomas Charles
4. FARADAY Michael
5. HALL Radclyffe
6. HOLL Francis Montague
7. HUGHES David Edward
8. LANDSEER Thomas
9. LILLYWHITE Frederick Willi
10. ROSA Carl August Nicholas
11. ROSSETTI Family
12. SAYERS Tom
13. TENNYSON Frederick
14. WOMBWELL George
15. WOOD Ellen
16. WYMARK Patrick Carl

Samuel Taylor COLERIDGE buried in St Michael's Crypt

NEW CEMETERY

1. ELIOT George
2. FOYLE Family
3. FRIESE GREENE William
4. HOLYOAKE George Jacob
5. LEWES George Henry
6. MARX Karl Heinrich
7. SPENCER Herbert

KENSAL GREEN

KENSAL GREEN CEMETERY

Underground: Kensal Green   Buses: 18, 52

Opened in 1833, Kensal Green was the first large commercial cemetery to maintain satisfactory standards of hygiene. This was particularly notable when compared to the graveyards of Inner London, which were in the most appalling condition and had been condemned by several journalists, including Dickens. It covers fifty-six acres. Among the famous buried here are Thomas Hood, Leigh Hunt, John Leech, William Mulready, William Thackeray, Anthony Trollope and the Brunels.

AINSWORTH, William Harrison (1805-82). Author of many popular novels, one of his earliest, *Rookwood,* showing a fine talent for descriptive writing. Two of his most famous novels are *Jack Sheppard* and *Old St Paul's.* Among his friends were Dickens, Thackeray, Landseer and Cruikshank.

ALBERY, James (1838-89). Dramatist and playwright. He produced many plays at the Lyceum, the most successful being *Two Roses,* with Sir Henry Irving in the leading role.

AUGUSTUS FREDERICK, Duke of Sussex (1773-1843). Sixth son of George III and Queen Charlotte. He strongly supported the progressive political policy. He was President of the Society of Arts in 1816 and Grand Master of the Freemasons, 1811. His sister SOFIA (d. 1848) is buried in the grave opposite. (Large monument)

BABBAGE, Charles (1792-1871). Mathematician and scientific mechanician. He was educated at Trinity College, Cambridge, and became a fellow of the Royal Society. His inventions included the forerunners of modern calculating machines and computers.

BALFE, Michael William (1808-70). Irish composer, violinist, singer and conductor of Italian opera. He was taught music by his father, who was organist at St George's Chapel, Windsor. In 1838 Balfe was commissioned to write librettos for Her Majesty's Theatre and one of these, *Falstaff,* contained some of his finest music.

BARNES, Thomas (1785-1841). Writer, and editor of *The Times.* He was educated first at Christ's Hospital (where one of his schoolfellows was Leigh Hunt), and then at Pembroke College, Cambridge. Barnes belonged to the literary circle which included Lamb and Hazlitt.

BARTOLOZZI, Gaetano Stefano (1757-1821). Engraver. Born in Rome, he led rather a Bohemian life, ran a musical and fencing academy in Paris, and eventually died in poverty. He was the son of Francesco Bartolozzi, and the father of Madame Vestris, the actress, who is also buried at Kensal Green. (See below).

BEATTY, Sir William, M.D. (d. 1842). Surgeon. He entered the Navy at an early age and saw much service throughout the world. He was for a time Physician to Greenwich Hospital. Beatty attended Lord Nelson after he received his mortal wound at the Battle of Trafalgar, and later published a book relating Nelson's death. He also retained the actual musket ball that inflicted the wound, and had it mounted in gold.

BEHNES, William (1795-1864). Sculptor. Son of a Hanoverian piano-maker, he was taught this craft, but later took drawing and sculpture lessons at the Royal Academy. He is best known for his portrait busts and child studies. Two of his busts, those of Sir William Follet and Dr Babington, were placed in Westminster Abbey and St Paul's, respectively. Behnes became bankrupt in 1861 and three years later was found dying in the street.

BENEDICT, Sir Julius (1804-85). Composer and conductor, born in Stuttgart. He accompanied Jenny Lind to America in 1850, and for many years conducted the Norwich Festival. He was the composer of *The Lily of Killarney*.

BIRKBECK, Dr George (1776-1841). Founder of technical and mechanical institutions. Birkbeck took his M.D. in 1799, and in 1800 he established courses of lectures—which developed into the Glasgow Mechanics' Institution—at a very low fee, for working men. He later set up practice as a physician in Finsbury Square. He was the founder of University College, London. His London Mechanics' Institution is now Birkbeck College.

BLONDIN, Charles (1824-97). His real name was Jean François Gravelet. He was an acrobat at the age of five and later became famous when he crossed the Niagara Falls on a tightrope. He repeated this performance several times, carrying a man on his shoulders, walking on stilts, in a sack, or pushing a wheelbarrow. Blondin later settled in England.

BRAHAM, John (c. 1774-1856). Tenor. A German Jew who studied singing in Italy and later appeared at Covent Garden and all the important opera houses in London. He also sang at the Three Choirs Festival at Gloucester.

BROOKS, Charles William Shirley (1816-74). Editor of *Punch* and author of several novels and volumes of humorous verse.

BRUNEL, Isambard Kingdom (1806-59). Civil engineer, son of Sir Marc Isambard Brunel. His greatest fame was obtained in the construction of very large ocean-going steamships, including the *Great Eastern*. He also planned the Clifton Suspension Bridge, 1829, and built most of the Great Western Railway.

BRUNEL, Sir Marc Isambard (1769-1849). Engineer. He was born in Normandy and educated at a seminary in Rouen. He then joined the navy and in 1793 emigrated to America where he became a civil engineer and architect. In 1799 he was appointed civil engineer of New York. He later came to England where he invented many devices for the improvement of docks and was responsible for the construction of the Thames tunnel (1825-43). Many setbacks and strains during this period led to an attack of partial paralysis and the end of his professional work. He was a fellow of the Royal Society, Member of the French Institute, Member of the Legion d'Honneur, etc.

BURTON, Decimus (1800-81). English architect. After training at the Royal Academy school, he went into practice at an early age and became a leading figure in the Classical revival. He designed many London buildings, including houses at Regent's Park, the old Charing Cross Hospital, and the Pimlico Arch at Hyde Park Corner. The Athenaeum Club in London is regarded as his masterpiece.

CALLCOTT, Sir Augustus Wall (1779-1844). Painter. Brother of John Callcott, the musician. He was a student at the Royal Academy, and the first picture which he exhibited there, a portrait, had great success. His later paintings were mainly landscapes and seascapes, some of which are in the Victoria and Albert Museum. His wife, Maria (1785-1842), also buried in Kensal Green, was a successful authoress of children's books.

CASSELL, John (1871-65). Publisher. Born in his father's inn, The Ring o'Bells, in Manchester. After a scanty education, he was apprenticed to a joiner, but in 1836, came to London where he sold tea, coffee and patent medicines. He read extensively and started writing, became his own publisher and developed it as a business. His publications included *Cassell's Illustrated Family Paper,* which had a very large circulation, and many educational books and standard classics. Cassell was known as a strict abstainer, but was rarely seen without a cigar.

COLLINS, William Wilkie (1824-89). Author. Called to the bar in 1851, published his first novel, *Antonia,* in 1850. He was a friend of Dickens and collaborated with him on *No Thoroughfare,* 1867, also contributing to Dickens's *Household Words* and *All the Year Round.* Collins wrote some twenty-six stories and novels, but his best known are *The Woman in White,* 1860, and *The Moonstone,* 1868.

COSTA, Sir Michael (1810-84). Conductor and composer. Born in Naples, he had some success as a composer in Italy before coming to England to produce his own opera, *Malek Adhel.* He was then appointed conductor of the Philharmonic concerts at Covent Garden. His most prominent works are two oratorios, *Eli* and *Naaman.* Costa was the first master of the art of the conductor, a role which hitherto had been taken by the first violinist or the pianist.

DANIELL, Thomas (1749-1840). Landscape painter. He served his apprenticeship as an heraldic painter, then became a student at the Royal Academy. After a visit to India he published views of Calcutta, and then set to work on *Oriental Scenery* which he completed in 1808. He was elected a member of the Royal Academy in 1799 and exhibited pictures there from 1772 to 1830. Fellow of the Royal Society.

DUCROW, Andrew (1793-1842). Circus rider who performed at Franconi's Circus in Paris. He produced the spectacle of *St George and the Dragon* at Drury Lane. Known as the King of Mimics. (One of the most impressive tombs, designed by John Cusworth)

DURHAM, Joseph, A.R.A. (1814-77). Sculptor. He exhibited at the Royal Academy in 1875. His subjects were mainly figures, many of his best being of boy-athletes.

DYER, George (1755-1841). Historian of Cambridge. Born in London—his father is said to have been a watchman at Wapping.

Educated at Christ's Hospital and at Emmanuel College, Cambridge. He returned to London in 1792, and contributed to magazines and to Valpy's edition of the classics in 141 volumes. His other works include some on the history of the University and colleges of Cambridge, poems and critical essays.

EASTLAKE, Sir Charles Lock (1793-1865). Landscape and portrait painter. President of the Royal Academy and Director of the National Gallery, Eastlake was one of the greatest authorities on art of his time and published many books on the subject. He spent many years in Italy and died there, but his body was brought back to England at the request of the Royal Academy. Among his best known works are *Byron's Dream* (in the National Gallery), *Pilgrims in Sight of Rome, Hagar and Ishmael, Christ blessing little Children* and *Christ weeping over Jerusalem.*

FORSTER, John (1812-76). Historian and biographer. His famous biography of Dickens was published in 1872. He was a friend of Leigh Hunt and Lamb and dramatic critic with the *Examiner.* (Buried with his sister Elizabeth)

GEORGE WILLIAM FREDERICK CHARLES, Duke of Cambridge (1819-1904). He was a grandson of George III and a Fieldmarshal and Commander of the British Army. He was personal Aide-de-Camp to Queen Victoria, 1882-95. He was connected with many charitable institutions such as the London Hospital and Christ's Hospital.

HANCOCK, Thomas (1786-1865). Founder of the India-rubber trade in England. In 1820 he took out a patent applying India-rubber springs to articles of dress, and in 1843 he first made 'vulcanized' India-rubber.

HARLEY, John Pritt (1786-1858). Comedian, actor and singer. As a young man he was apprenticed to a linendraper in Ludgate Hill. During his stage career he appeared with Macready at Covent

Garden and was a member of Charles Kean's company. He was known as 'Fat Jack' on account of his thinness. Harley had a seizure whilst on stage at the Prince's Theatre, his last words being from *A Midsummer Night's Dream*—'I feel an exposition of sleep come upon me'. He had a passion for collecting walking sticks and more than three hundred were sold after his death.

HOBHOUSE, John Cam, Baron Broughton De Gyfford (1786-1869). Statesman. Educated at Trinity College, Cambridge, where he founded the Whig Club. He was a friend of Byron and was best man at his wedding in 1815. Hobhouse was held guilty of a breach of privilege by the House of Commons and committed to Newgate in 1819, where he remained until the dissolution of Parliament. After his release he again stood for Parliament at Westminster and was elected. He was the author of many books on travel and politics.

HOGARTH, Mary Scott (1819-1837). Dickens's young sister-in-law. It is said that Dickens had a greater love for her than anybody else in his life, and that he never fully recovered from his grief at her death.

HOLWORTHY, James (d. 1841). Member of the Society of Painters in Watercolours, and a friend of Turner. He was the son-in-law of Joseph Wright, the painter.

HOOD, Thomas (1799-1845). Poet. Hood began by writing for local newspapers and then became articled to his uncle, an engraver, an occupation which proved too trying for his delicate health. He became assistant sub-editor of the *London Magazine*, to which he contributed verse. He began *Hood's Magazine* in 1844. Among his acquaintances were De Quincey, Hazlitt and Charles Lamb.

HUME, Joseph (1777-1855). Radical politician. He entered the East India Company in the medical section and became an army surgeon. Later he was elected M.P. for Aberdeen, and promoted the repeal of the Corn Laws, 1834. He was very concerned with public expenditure.

HUNT, James Henry Leigh (1784-1859). Author, essayist, critic and poet. He was a clerk to his brother, an attorney at the War Office, and was convicted with him to two years imprisonment for attacks on the Prince Regent. While in prison he decorated his cell with roses and a trellis, formed a friendship with Byron, edited the *Examiner* and also wrote *The Descent of Liberty*. It was Hunt who introduced the public to the works of Shelley and Keats. He lived in the same house as Shelley in Pisa, was present at his cremation and wrote the epitaph on his tomb. Hunt had a large circle of famous friends, including Carlyle. A portrait of him by Haydon is in the National Portrait Gallery.

JAMESON, Mrs Anna Brownell (1794-1860). Authoress. Born in Dublin, the daughter of D. Brownell Murphy, the Irish miniaturist, she came to England in 1798. She was a friend of Ottilie von Goethe and of Lady Byron (although they later quarrelled). Her best known works are *Sacred and Legendary Art*, and *Characteristics of Women*. A bust of her by John Gibson is in the National Portrait Gallery.

LEECH, John (1817-64). Illustrator. Educated at Charterhouse. His genius was discovered at an early age by Flaxman. Leech was distinguished for his excellent anatomical drawings. He illustrated *Punch*, amongst other works, but was especially famous for his illustration of Dickens's works. A friend of Thackeray.

LESLIE, Charles Robert, R.A. (1794-1859). Author, artist, painter and biographer of Constable and Reynolds. He was the eldest son of American parents, and his father was a personal friend of Benjamin Franklin. In 1848 he was made Professor of Painting at the Royal Academy. He is especially famed for his humorous works. (Large family tomb)

LISTON, John (c. 1776-1846). Comic actor who appeared at Covent Garden and in supporting roles with Sarah Siddons. He was the original Paul Pry in John Poole's play of that name.

LOCKHART, John Gibson (1794-1854). He was the biographer of Sir Walter Scott. He married Scott's daughter Sophia (see below) in 1820. He contributed to *Blackwood's Magazine* and edited the *Quarterly Review*. He published a *Life of Burns,* 1828 and also his *Life of Scott* in 1838. He is buried beside his wife.

LONG, John St John (1798-1834). Quack doctor who set up in London and had a fashionable practice. He was twice tried for manslaughter after the deaths of his patients.

LOUDON, John Claudius (1783-1843). Landscape gardener and author of numerous books on gardening. His works include a book on the laying out of public squares, an *Encyclopedia of Plants* and an *Encyclopedia of Agriculture.*

LOVER, Samuel (1797-1868). Song writer, novelist and painter. A friend of Dickens. He painted miniature portraits, wrote ballads and was associated with Dickens in founding *Bentley's Magazine.*

MAYHEW, Henry (1812-87). Founder and joint editor of *Punch.* He was the author of *London Labour and the London Poor,* an encyclopedia of the petty trades of the people of London. He also drew up tables of crime and illegitimate births, and wrote humorous novels.

William Mulready

MULREADY, William, R.A. (1786-1863). Artist and illustrator. He was born at Ennis, County Clare, and became a student at the Royal Academy in 1800. The books which he illustrated include Lamb's *Tales from Shakespeare* and *The Vicar of Wakefield*. Of his paintings, the best known are probably *The Wolf and the Lamb*, which belongs to the Queen and *Choosing the Wedding Gown*, which is in the Victoria and Albert Museum. (Tomb by G. Sykes)

MURRAY, John (1778-1843). Publisher. Murray started as a publisher and book-seller in his father's business in Fleet Street. His first publication of note was *The Revolutionary Plutarch* in 1803. He purchased a house at 50, Albemarle Street in 1812 and published the works of Jane Austen, Scott, Southey, and Palgrave, to name but a few. It is as Byron's publisher, however, that he is most famous.

MUSGRAVE, Thomas (1788-1860). Archbishop of York. He was educated in Richmond, Yorkshire, and between 1823 and 1837 held the college livings of Lover, St Mary's Cambridge and Bottisham. He obtained the See of York in 1848 and was also an active county magistrate.

O'CONNOR, Feargus (1794-1855). Chartist leader. He advocated peasant proprietorship and founded the National Land Company to buy estates and let them to subscribers by ballot. He was pronounced insane in 1852.

PELLEGRINI, Carlo (1839-89). Cari-caturist. Born in Italy, where he became a volunteer in Garibaldi's army. He came to England in 1864. He made hundreds of humorous drawings of famous men of his time, and was responsible for the caricatures in *Vanity Fair*. He always signed his work 'Ape'.

PHILLIP, John (1817-67). Painter of portraits and general subjects. He is said to have started as a painter of signs and houses. Lord Panmure brought him to London, where he studied painting. He was influenced by Velasquez. Elected member of the Royal Academy in 1859.

PICKERING, William (1796-1854). Publisher. He set up business in Lincoln's Inn Fields, and later the Aldine Press in Chancery Lane, where he made his reputation with an edition of the English poets in fifty-three volumes. He was in financial difficulties when he died.

PRAED, Winthrop Mackworth (1802-39). Poet. Educated at Trinity College, Cambridge, where he read classics with Macaulay and was a contributor to the *Quarterly Magazine*. In 1827 he was elected a Fellow at Trinity. He stood for Parliament and was eventually successful in 1834. Praed wrote prose and verse for the *Morning Post*, and his first collection of poems appeared in New York in 1844.

REID, Mayne (1818-83). Novelist, originally called Thomas Mayne Reid. He worked as correspondent of the *New York Times*, and wrote many adventure novels based on his experiences in Mexico. A friend of Edgar Allan Poe.

ROSS, Sir John, K.C.B. (1777-1856). Rear-admiral and Arctic navigator. Ross made several journeys to the Arctic, once having to abandon ship because of ice and live in a hut built from the wreck, while another voyage was remarkable for the length of time spent ice-bound. He was knighted in 1834 and awarded various gold medals. He later became Consul in Stockholm. He published *A Voyage of Discovery*.

SCOTT, Anne (1803-33) and Charlotte Sophia Lockhart (1799-1837). Daughters of Sir Walter Scott. Also John Gibson LOCKHART, Scott's son-in-law (see above).

SCRIVEN, Edward (1775-1841). Engraver who executed portraits for various publications, including the *British Gallery of Portraits*, 1809-17.

SIEVIER, Robert William (1794-1865). Sculptor, who exhibited at the Royal Academy, 1822-44. He worked mainly on monuments and busts. His work can be seen in St George's Chapel, Windsor, Gloucester, etc.

SMEATON, John (1724-92). Civil engineer. He showed great engineering promise as a boy when he constructed working models of steam engines. His main work was on bridges in Scotland, but his greatest fame was achieved by his construction of the third Eddystone lighthouse (finished in 1759 and used for more than 100 years). He also carried out work on the Forth and Clyde Canal. There is a portrait of him in the National Portrait Gallery.

SMIRKE, Robert, R.A. (1752-1845). Painter and illustrator. He illustrated Boydell's *Shakespeare Gallery* and Bowyer's *History of England.*

STANFIELD, Clarkson, R.A. (1793-1867). The majority of his pictures were taken from sketches he made on his frequent travels to the continent. Some of his works are at the National Gallery and at the Victoria and Albert Museum. Stanfield was a friend of Thackeray, Dickens and Landseer.

STEEL, Alan Gibson (1858-1914). Cricketer and barrister. Steel played for Cambridge, where his University team beat the first Australian team to play in England in 1878. He was a very accurate slow bowler, noted for his footwork and power in hitting as a batsman, and was thought to be second only to W.G. Grace. He was President of the Marylebone Cricket Club, 1902. He was called to the bar in 1883.

STEWART, Charles James (1775-1837). Bishop of Quebec, 1826-37. He was born in England and educated at Corpus Christi College, Oxford. He went to Canada as a missionary.

STRANG, William, R.A. (1859-1921). Painter and etcher. He was a pupil of Alphonse Legros. He produced over 700 etchings and also illustrated books.

THACKERAY, William Makepeace (1811-63). Novelist. Born in Calcutta and educated at Charterhouse (where he was impressed by the brutality of the English public school), and at Trinity College, Cambridge. His best known work, *Vanity Fair,* was published in 1847-8. Other works include the *History of Pendennis* and *The Newcomes.* He was also a contributor to *Punch.* There is a portrait of him in the National Portrait Gallery and another in the Garrick Club.

TIETJENS or TITIENS, Teresa Caroline Johanna (1831-77). Singer. Born in Hamburg of Hungarian parents, she was one of the greatest mezzo-sopranos of her time.

TINDAL, Sir Nicholas Conyngham (1776-1846). Chief Justice of the Common Pleas. He was Tory M.P. for Wigtown Burghs, then Harwich, and later representative of the University of Cambridge. He was appointed Chief Justice in 1829. There is a portrait of him in the National Portrait Gallery.

TROLLOPE, Anthony (1815-82). Author and novelist. Trollope was a clerk in the Post Office, and his civil service background was put to use in many novels. He clashed with Sir Rowland Hill (head of the Post Office) and resigned in 1864. He claimed responsibilty for the introduction of the postal pillar-box. His best known works are *Barchester Towers, Last Chronicle of Barset* and *Phineas Finn.*

TURTON, Thomas (1780-1864). Bishop of Ely. He was educated at Cambridge and was Professor of Mathematics. He was recommended by Sir Robert Peel to the See of Ely in 1845. Turton was a controversial and vigorous writer, and also composed several pieces of church music.

VESTRIS, Madame Lucia Elizabeth (1797-1856). Actress. She was the daughter of Bartolozzi (see above),the engraver. She had great success as an opera-singer (contralto) and as an actress. Deserted by her first husband, a dancer and ballet-master, she later married Charles Mathews, an actor, whom she helped to manage Covent Garden and later the Lyceum. There is a portrait of her in the Victoria and Albert Museum and another in the Garrick Club.

WARD, James, R.A. (1769-1859). Painter and engraver. His subjects were principally animals and domestic scenes, which he painted in a vigorous style. He was commissioned to paint cattle by the Board of Agriculture. One of his best known paintings, the *Gordale Scar,* is in the Tate Gallery.

WINGFIELD, Major Walter Clopton (1833-1912) Inventor of 'Sphairistike' (1874), early form of lawn tennis played on a hourglass-shaped court.

Kensal Green (Ducrow's tomb,left)

SKETCH PLAN OF KENSAL GREEN CEMETERY

1. AINSWORTH William Harrison
2. AUGUSTUS FREDERICK,Duke of Sussex
3. BABBAGE Charles
4. BALFE Michael William
5. BARNES Thomas
6. BEHNES William
7. BENEDICT Sir Julius
8. BIRKBECK Dr George
9. BLONDIN Charles
10. BRAHAM John
11. BROOKS Charles William Shirley

12. BRUNEL Isambard Kingdom
13. BRUNEL Sir Marc Isambard
14. BURTON Decimus
15. CALLCOTT Sir Augustus Wall
16. CASSELL John
17. COLLINS William Wilkie
18. DANIELL Thomas
19. DUCROW Andrew
20. DURHAM Joseph
21. DYER George
22. EASTLAKE Sir Charles Lock

23. FORSTER John
24. GEORGE, Duke of Cambridge
25. HANCOCK Thomas
26. HOGARTH Mary Scott
27. HOLWORTHY James
28. HOOD Thomas
29. HUME Joseph
30. HUNT James Henry Leigh
31. JAMESON Anna Brownell
32. LEECH John
33. LESLIE Charles Robert

34. LISTON John
25. LOUDON John Claudius
36. LOVER Samuel
37. MULREADY William
38. MURRAY John
39. O'CONNOR Feargus
40. PHILLIP John
41. PICKERING William
42. ROSS Sir John
43. SCRIVEN Edward
44. SIEVIER Robert William

45. SMIRKE Robert
46. STRANG William
47. THACKERAY William Makepeace
48. TIETJENS Teresa Caroline Johanna
49. TINDAL Sir Nicholas Conyngham
50. TROLLOPE Anthony
51. VESTRIS Lucia Elizabeth
52. WARD James
53. WINGFIELD, Major Walter Clopton

C. CATACOMBS

Entrance to St Mary's
R.C. Cemetery

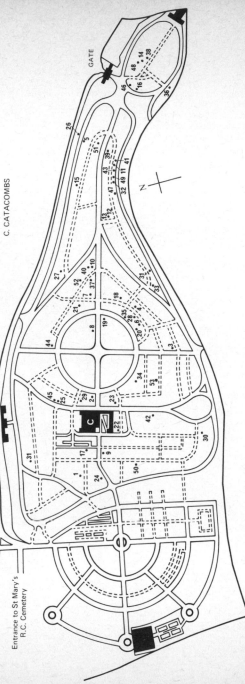

KENSAL GREEN

ST MARY'S ROMAN CATHOLIC CEMETERY

Underground: Kensal Green

Bus: 18

The first interment in a common grave in this burial ground was in 1858. There were vaults here before that date, however. The burial ground, which adjoins the Kensal Green Cemetery, covers twenty-six acres, and burials there include those of St Mary's clergy, nuns and foreign families.

BARBIROLLI, Sir John (1899-1970). Famous conductor and musician. Of Italian and French parentage. He founded the Barbirolli Chamber Orchestra in 1925, and was conductor of the New York Philharmonic Orchestra, and the Hallé Orchestra. He received many awards in Europe and America.

BONAPARTE, Louis Lucien (1813-91). Nephew of Napoleon I. He was a phonetician and philologist who studied the Basque language. He was made a Prince in 1863 by Napoleon III. He lived in London for many years and died in Paddington.

GRANVILLE, Christine, G.M., O.B.E., Croix de Guerre avec Palmes (1915-52). She was a heroine of the Second World War. Her real name was Countess Krystyna Skarbek, and she was born near Warsaw. She became Miss Poland in 1933. During the war she worked for the French Resistance movement and helped in the escapes of many Allied soldiers and airmen. For her wartime achievements she received more decorations than any other woman. She was murdered in London by a former lover.

HARDING, Gilbert Charles (1907-60). Television personality, known for his outspoken views and for his appearances in quiz programmes—e.g. *What's My Line?*

HENDERSON, Dick (1891-1958). Comedian who appeared in music halls. Father of Dickie Henderson.

MANCINI, Al (1903-68). Boxer.

MEYNELL, Alice Christiana Gertrude (1847-1922). Poet and journalist. Although she had eight children she still found time for writing. Her first book of poetry was published in 1875, and she wrote essays on Dickens and the Brontës. She was a great friend of Coventry Patmore.

O'CONNOR, Thomas Power (1848-1929). Statesman, orator and journalist. He was an Irish patriot and M.P. for the Scotland division of Liverpool, 1885-1929. In 1917 he became the first President of the Board of Film Censors.

Christine Granville

PANIZZI, Sir Anthony (1797-1879). Principal Librarian of the British Museum and originator of the idea of the Reading Room. He was born in Italy, and was much involved with Italian political political problems. In 1823 he was implicated in a plot against the Modenese Government and fled to Britain.

SEACOLE, Mary (1805-81). Nurse, noted for her care of the wounded on the battlefields of the Crimea and of the sick and needy in Jamaica.

THOMPSON, Francis (1859-1907). Poet. Born in Preston. He was educated for the Roman Catholic priesthood, then trained in medicine. He failed to qualify as a doctor, fell into extreme poverty and took to opium. After the publication of his first book, *Poems*, in 1893, he was hailed as a mystical poet. He wrote the lives of St Ignatius Loyola and John Baptist de la Galle. Died of consumption.

TUSSAUD, Buried here are several members of the family of Marie Tussaud, who founded the famous waxworks.
(in chapel vaults)

KENSINGTON

Fulham Road   BROMPTON CEMETERY

Underground: Earl's Court or Fulham Broadway   Buses: 14, 30

Founded in 1831 and consecrated in 1840, it was named the West of London and Westminster Cemetery. It covers about thirty-eight acres and was one of the earliest large cemeteries opened to relieve the overcrowded churchyards of London. An interesting feature of this cemetery is the octagonal chapel with colonnades. Buried here are Emmeline Pankhurst and Gentleman John Jackson, the pugilist.

BONOMI, Joseph, the Younger (1796-1878). Sculptor. He worked under Nollekens. Curator of Sir John Soane's Museum at Lincoln's Inn Fields in London, 1861-78.

BORROW, George Henry (1803-1881). Author and philogist. Born in Norfolk. He began his career as the articled clerk of a solicitor. He toured through England and Europe, and related his experiences in *Lavengro* and *Romany Rye*. He won acclaim for *Gypsies in Spain* and the *Bible in Spain*. He revolted against the genteel writing of his time and his works introduced a new approach to the open air life, his characters being drawn from the ale houses and bare-fisted boxing rings. He died at Oulton, Suffolk, and is buried here with his mother.

BUCKLAND, Francis Trevelyan (1826-80). Naturalist. He studied surgery at St George's Hospital, London and he was author of *Curiosities of Natural History*.

BYRON, Henry James (1834-84). Dramatist and theatre manager. He was a medical student in London, but wrote farces and comedies for the stage, and also a novel, *Paid in Full*, 1865.

CHENERY, Thomas (1826-84). Editor of *The Times* and a barrister. He was an excellent linguist and was Professor of Arabic at Oxford.

COLE, Sir Henry (1808-82). Founder of the South Kensington Art and Science Museum. He painted in water-colours and made engravings for book illustrations.

He was an official at Christ's Hospital.

COLLINS, Charles Allston (1828-73). Pre-Raphaelite painter and author. He exhibited at the Royal Academy and wrote novels.

COOKE, Thomas Potter (1786-1864). Actor. The son of a London surgeon. He appeared on the London stage at the Lyceum in 1820 and acted in Paris.

COOMBES, Robert Albert (1808-60). Champion sculler of the Thames and Tyne. He worked on the Thames as a waterman. Although only 5ft 8 in in height, he was constantly matched against men superior in strength and size, but by his skill always proved victorious. He died in a lunatic asylum in Kent. (Monument. The epitaph says 'Fare thee well my trim-built wherry. Oars, coat and badge, farewell')

Robert Coombes

CROCKER J.P. (1834-69). One of the members of the original music hall singing group, the Christie Minstrels.

CROKER, Thomas Crofton (1798-1854). Irish antiquary. He helped to found the Camden Society, 1839, and the British Archaeological Association, 1843. He published songs and stories about Ireland.

DAVISON, James William (1813-85). Journalist and music critic. He studied at the Royal College of Music and became music critic of *The Times,* 1846-85.

DONALDSON, Thomas Leverton (1795-1885). Architect and author. He was a silver medallist at the Royal Academy, 1817, President of the Institute of Architects, 1864, and Professor of Architecture at University College, London, 1841-64. He designed churches and large houses in London.

John Jackson

FOX, William Johnson (1786-1864). Preacher and politician. Also a writer—he contributed to the *Westminster Review* and wrote the Anti-Corn Law League's address to the nation, 1840. A friend of Bulmer Macready.

FOY, Tom (1866-1917). Music hall comedian, born in Yorkshire.

GODWIN, George (1815-88). Architect. He won the Architects' Prize for an essay on concrete in 1835, and a gold medal from the Institute of Architects in 1881. He was an active member of the Royal Commission on Housing for the Working Classes, 1884.

GOLDING, Dr Benjamin (1793-1863). The founder of Charing Cross Hospital, where he was Director until 1862.

HARRIS, Sir Augustus Henry Glossop (1852-1896). Theatre manager and manager of Covent Garden.

JACKSON, John (1769-1845). Pugilist ('Gentleman John'). He was the champion of England, 1795-1803, and later opened a boxing school in Bond Street, London, where one of his well-known pupils was Lord Byron. (Large monument)

KAY-SHUTTLEWORTH, Sir James Phillips (1804-77). The founder of English popular education. He wrote books on health and was also joint founder of Battersea training college for pupil-teachers. He was Vice-chairman of the central relief committee during the Lancashire cotton famine, 1861-5.

KEELEY, Robert (1793-1869). Actor. He appeared on stage at Covent Garden and the Lyceum, acting with Madame Vestris, Macready, Strutt (in Dickens's plays) and Kean.

LAMBERT, Percy E. (1881-1913). Pioneer of motor-racing at Brooklands. The first man to cover one hundred miles in one hour. Killed by accident at Brooklands racing track while attempting further records.

LOW, A.M. (1888-1956). President of the British Institute of Engineering Technology. He invented a system of radio signalling, an electrical rocket control (1917) and a television system. He was the author of many books on engineering.

MERIVALE, Herman (1806-74). Barrister, and Under-secretary for India. Professor of Political Economy at Oxford, 1837. Author of *Historical Studies,* 1865, and the *Life of Sir Henry Lawrence,* 1872.

MURCHISON, Sir Roderick Impey (1792-1871). Geologist. He served in the army and then became interested in geology, particularly in a type of red sandstone rock, which he named Silurian. In 1835 he published *The Silurian System.* He was President of the Royal Geographical Society in 1843. He travelled all over the world and made a special study of the Ural mountains.

NEILSON, Lilian Adelaide (1848-80). Actress. Her real name was Elizabeth Ann Brown, and she once worked as a millhand and also as a barmaid. She gave a notable performance as Juliet in 1865 and as a tragedienne had few rivals.

NICHOLSON, Francis (1753-1844). Water-colour painter and author of works on this subject. He brought a stronger quality of depth of tone to the art of water-colour in light tints.

NOBLE, Matthew (1818-76). Sculptor, mainly of busts. He exhibited at the Royal Academy, 1845-76.

PALLISER, Sir William (1830-82). Inventor, mainly in the sphere of guns. He converted smooth bores into rifled guns, and in 1863 patented a chilled cast-iron shot, the 'Palliser shot', which at that time superseded steel projectiles.

PANKHURST, Emmeline (1858-1928). Suffragette. The daughter of a calico-printer, she joined the Independent

Emmeline Pankhurst

Labour Party in 1892. She founded the Women's Social and Political Union, and was imprisoned about eight times for her activities as the militant leader of the Suffragettes. In 1918 she joined the Conservative Party. Her tactics as a Suffragette included smashing windows, arson and hunger strikes.

PENTON, Stephen (1793-1873). Traveller. He was Consul-general in Peru in 1827. He made surveys of the Bolivian Andes, a place rarely visited by Europeans and was the first to measure many of these mountains. He also edited books on travel.

RICHARDS, Henry Brinley (1819-85). Composer and pianist. Besides many piano pieces he also wrote the song *God bless the Prince of Wales.*

ROMILLY, John, 1st Baron Romilly (1802-74). Master of the Rolls and Privy Councillor.

SMITH, Albert Richard (1816-60). Author. One-time student at the Middlesex Hospital. He contributed to *Punch* and also wrote several novels.

SMITH, Sir Francis Pettit (1808-74). The inventor of the four-bladed screw-propeller for steamships. He was knighted in 1871.

SNOW, John (1813-1858). An anaesthetist who trained as a surgeon. He discovered that cholera is communicated by contaminated water and was the first man in Britain to improve ether for use as an anaesthetizing agent. (It had already been used in America.) He also experimented with chloroform.

TAUBER, Richard (1891-1948). Famous singer and conductor. He was born in Austria, but became a British subject in 1940. A tenor, he appeared in opera and operetta, on stage and in films. He conducted and sang in guest performances and concerts all over the world.

TAYLOR, Tom (1817-80). Dramatist and editor of *Punch*. He contributed to several newspapers including the *Daily News, The Times* and the *Graphic,* and was the author of a biography of Haydon.

TERRISS, William (1847-97). Actor. After appearing at the Prince of Wales Theatre. Birmingham, he acted many Shakespearean roles on the London stage and accompanied Irving to America. He was murdered while entering the Adelphi Theatre, London.

THESIGER, Alfred Henry (1838-80). Lord Justice of Appeal and Privy Councillor, 1877-80.

THOMAS, Brandon (1850-1914). Actor and playwright. His farce, *Charley's Aunt,* produced in 1892, ran for 1 466 performances, and has been revived many times.

VAUX, William Sandys Wright (1818-85). Antiquary. British Museum Keeper of Coins and Medals. He catalogued Bodleian coins and was the author of works on Assyrian, Greek and Egyptian art and history.

WARNEFORD, Lieutenant, V.C. (1891-1915). First World War aviator who destroyed a Zeppelin in mid-air near Bruges in 1915. He was later killed flying near Paris.

WEBSTER, Benjamin Nottingham (1797-1882). Actor, ballet-master, musician and clown. He generally played in low comedy, but also built up a reputation as a dramatist. He was manager of the Haymarket and Adelphi Theatres.

WILLIAMS, Sir William Fenwick (1800-83). General, Royal Artillery. He held Kars against the Russians and won the Battle of Kars in 1855. He was Commander-in-Chief of Gibraltar, 1870-76, and Constable of the Tower of London, 1881.

SKETCH PLAN OF BROMPTON CEMETERY

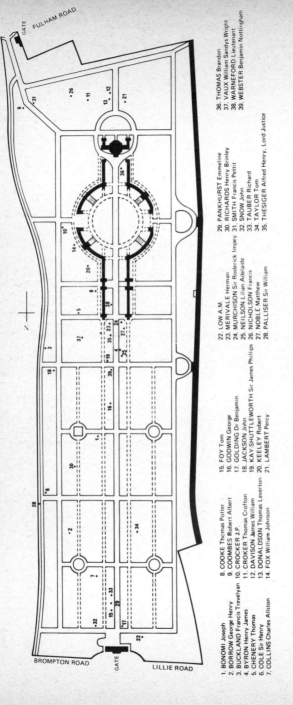

1. BONOMI Joseph
2. BORROW George Henry
3. BUCKLAND Francis Trevelyan
4. BYRON Henry James
5. CHENERY Thomas
6. COLE Sir Henry
7. COLLINS Charles Allston
8. COOKE Thomas Potter
9. COOMBES Robert Albert
10. CROKER J.P.
11. CROKER Thomas Crofton
12. DAVISON James William
13. DONALDSON Thomas Leverton
14. FOX William Johnson

15. FOY Tom
16. GODWIN George
17. GOLDING Dr Benjamin
18. JACKSON John
19. KAY SHUTTLEWORTH Sir James Philips
20. KEELEY Robert
21. LAMBERT Percy

22. LOW A.M.
23. MERIVALE Herman
24. MURCHISON Sir Roderick Impey
25. NEILSON Lilian Adelaide
26. NICHOLSON Francis
27. NOBLE Matthew
28. PALLISER Sir William

29. PANKHURST Emmeline
30. RICHARDS Henry Brinley
31. SMITH Francis Pettit
32. SNOW John
33. TAUBER Richard
34. TAYLOR Tom
35. THESIGER Alfred Henry, Lord Justice

36. THOMAS Brandon
37. VAUX William Sandys Wright
38. WARNEFORD Lieutenant
39. WEBSTER Benjamin Nottingham

NORWOOD HIGH STREET
NORWOOD CEMETERY

Buses: 68, 172, 196

Originally called the South Metropolitan Cemetery, this cemetery was established after Kensal Green had been formed in the west of London. Consecrated in 1837, it covers about forty acres. It was designed by Sir William Tite, who is buried in the vaults. An interesting feature here is that there is a Greek section in the north-east part of the main cemetery. Among those who are buried here are Sir Henry Bessemer and Mrs Beeton.

In 1966 this cemetery was acquired by Lambeth Borough Council.

BEETON, Mrs (1836-65). Originally Isabella Mary Mayson. Author of the famous household and cookery books. She married a book publisher, Samuel Orchart Beeton (1831-77), who is also buried here. He was the first English publisher of Harriet Beecher Stowe's *Uncle Tom's Cabin.*

BESSEMER, Sir Henry (1813-98). Engineer and inventor. He discovered the process for making inexpensive and plentiful steel from pig-iron, and this method, the Bessemer steel process, was widely used in the USA. He also improved the type-setting machine and made a solar furnace and a large telescope.

CINQUEVALLI, Paul (1859-1918). Polish music hall clown and juggler, who performed at the Covent Garden Theatre.

COW, Peter Brusey (d. 1890). Inventor of Cow rubber products.

COX, David, the Younger (1809-1885). Water-colour painter. He was the only child of David Cox, the Elder, the more famous painter. He was not as talented as his father. He possessed a large collection of his father's works. Died in Streatham.

CUBITT, Thomas (1788-1855). Builder who started his working life as a ship's carpenter. He did much building in London, including the east front of Buckingham Palace.

CUBITT, Sir William (1785-1861). Civil engineer. He invented the treadmill in 1818 and also self-regulating sails for windmills. He constructed docks at Cardiff and was a consultant engineer for the French railways. He also constructed the Berlin waterworks.

DOULTON, Sir Henry (1820-97). Potter. He entered his father's business at Lambeth in 1835. He developed 'sgraffito' pottery which became very popular. He was knighted in 1887.

JERROLD, Douglas William (1803-57). Author and playwright. He started his acting career when still a child, but made his reputation as a playwright with *Black-eyed Susan.* Several of his plays were produced at Drury Lane. In 1845 he started *Douglas Jerrold's Magazine* and in 1846, *Douglas Jerrold's Newspaper.* He also contributed to *Punch* and had a reputation as a wit.

MANTELL, Gideon Algernon (1790-1852). Geologist. Son of a bootmaker, he was apprenticed to a surgeon. He made a study of natural history and his book *The Wonders of Geology* was published in 1838.

MARSDEN, William (1796-1867). Surgeon who founded the Royal Free Hospital, where the poor could be admitted without charge. He also founded Brompton Cancer Hospital.

MAXIM, Sir Hiram Stevens (1840-1916). Engineer and inventor who worked in America. He came to England and opened a workshop in London in 1882. He was naturalised in 1900, knighted,

1901. Among his inventions: a rapid-firing machine-gun adopted by the Services, and a steam-driven flying machine.

NAPIER, Sir William Francis Patrick (1785-1860). General, and historian of the Peninsular War. This work was highly regarded and was translated into five languages.

PROUT, Samuel (1783-1852). Water-colour painter. Most of his work is of landscape in the south-west of England, but he also produced a series depicting Continental streets and market-places.

REACH, Angus Bethune (1821-56). Journalist. He worked first for the *Illustrated London News,* and in 1849 joined the staff of *Punch.* He was the author of *Sketches of London Life and Character,* 1858.

ROBSON, Thomas Frederick (c. 1822-64). An actor whose real name was Brownhill. Before joining the acting profession he worked as a copperplate engraver. He was particularly talented at farce. In 1851 he played Bottom in *A Midsummer Night's Dream* and in 1853 joined the Olympic company.

SPURGEON, Charles Haddon (1834-92). Preacher. He became a Baptist in 1850, and came to London in 1854. His preaching was very popular, and he ministered at the Metropolitan Tabernacle until his death. He was an ardent Calvinist. His sermons were published at the rate of one per week, and he also published *John Ploughman's Talks* and the *Treasury of David.*

TALFOURD, Sir Thomas Noon (1795-1854). Judge and author. He published plays and dramatic criticism, and also wrote articles for the *Quarterly Review.* His acquaintances included Lamb, Wordsworth and Coleridge.

TATE, Sir Henry (1819-99). A merchant who was born and worked at a sugar refinery in Liverpool. He patented a device for cutting sugar into cubes. He founded the firm of Henry Tate and left vast sums of money for the founding of hospitals and the Tate Gallery, London.

TURNER, Sharon (1768-1847). Historian and attorney. He studied Icelandic and Anglo-Saxon literature, his chief work being a *History of England from the Earliest Period to the Norman Conquest,* 1799-1805.

WOODINGTON, William Frederick (1806-93). Sculptor and painter. His signature was found on the stone lion which used to stand on top of the brewery on the South Bank—now the Royal Festival Hall site.

SKETCH PLAN OF NORWOOD CEMETERY

1. BEETON Mrs
2. BEETON Samuel Orchart
3. CINQUEVALLI Paul
4. COW Peter Brusey
5. CUBITT Thomas
6. DOULTON Sir Henry
7. JERROLD Douglas William
8. MANTELL Gideon Algernon
9. MARSDEN William
10. MAXIM Sir Hiram Stevens
11. NAPIER Sir William Francis Patr
12. REACH Angus Bethune
13. ROBSON Thomas Frederick
14. SPURGEON Charles Haddon
15. TALFOURD Sir Thomas Noon
16. TATE Sir Henry
17. TURNER Sharon
18. WOODINGTON William Frederic

GATE

STOKE NEWINGTON CHURCH STREET

ABNEY PARK CEMETERY

Bus: 73

This cemetery was opened in May 1840. The architect was William Hosking, later Professor of Architecture and Engineering Construction at King's College, London. One monument here is particularly notable—a standing figure of Isaac Watts by Baily, although Watts is, in fact, buried in Bunhill Fields.

BARBOULD, Anna Letitia (1743-1825). Writer, *née* Aikin, who wrote poems and hymns. She founded a boys' school at Palgrave in Suffolk.

BOOTH, William (1829-1912). Known as General Booth, he was the founder of the Salvation Army. His wife, Catherine Mumford (1829-90), is also buried here.

FLEETWOOD, Bridget (d. 1662). Eldest daughter of Oliver Cromwell and widow of Henry Ireton, she later married General Fleetwood. (Buried under the church)

HONE, William (1780-1842). Author and bookseller who established a shop in Ludgate Hill. In 1817 he was prosecuted for his *Political Litany,* but was acquitted. He was the author of the *Political House that Jack Built* (illustrated by Cruikshank) and other works, and the editor of Stratt's *Sports and Pastimes.*

OFFOR, George (1787-1864). Editor and biographer of Bunyan. He possessed a collection of early English Bibles and psalters, but most of his books were burnt in a fire at Sotheby's in 1865.

OUR SWEET CONNIE,
DIED AT EASTER 1901
AGED 14 MONTHS.
"OF SUCH IS THE KINGDOM OF GOD"

ALSO ALICE EVANS,
MOTHER OF THE ABOVE
WHO FELL ASLEEP 23 DEC. 1938
AGED 69 YEARS

WEST HAMPSTEAD

Fortune Green Road

WEST HAMPSTEAD CEMETERY

Underground: West Hampstead

Buses: 13, 26, 113, 159

This burial ground, opened in 1876, has the look of a country cemetery, quite unlike Kensal Green or Brompton Cemetery. The chapel and lodge were designed by Charles Bell. Among those buried here are Marie Lloyd, Kate Greenaway and Josph Lister.

BAYNES, Thomas Spencer (1823-87). Philosopher. He was the editor of the *Edinburgh Guardian*, 1850-54, and Professor of Logic, Metaphysics and English Literature at St Andrews University, 1864.

BLAIR, Sir Robert (1859-1935). First education officer for London. He was President of the British Association Education Section in 1920.

BRAIN, Dennis (1921-57). He was principal French-horn for the Philharmonia Orchestra from 1946. He played all over the world and music was written for him by Britten, etc. He died in a car accident.

COOPER, Gladys, D.B.E. (1888-1971). Actress. Born at Lewisham, she began her career at the age of seventeen, becoming one of England's most popular actresses, playing in many stage comedies. She also appeared in films.

CREMER, Sir William Randal (1838-1908). English politician. He started work as a carpenter and became a prominent trade unionist and pacifist. He was Secretary of the International Arbitration League for thirty-seven years. Opposed to class warfare, he resigned when the committee declared for revolution. He was awarded the Nobel Peace Prize in 1903.

ERICHSEN, Sir John Eric (1818-96). Surgeon. Born in Copenhagen, he became Surgeon Extraordinary to Queen Victoria.

FERRANTI, Sebastian Ziani de (1864-1930). Electrical engineer and inventor of several types of dynamos and alternatives. He became President of the Institute of Electrical Engineers. He died in Zürich.

FISHER, Andrew (1862-1928). Privy Councillor. Born in Scotland, he went to Australia in 1885, where he became leader of the Australian Labour Party and Prime Minister of Australia, 1908-9, 1910-13 and 1914-15. He was High Commissioner for Australia in London, 1916-21.

FLETCHER, Bannister (1833-99). Architect of many public buildings and district surveyor of West Newington and part of Lambeth. Author of *A History of Architecture on the Comparative Method,* 1896.

FRANKAU, Pamela (1908-67). Novelist and journalist, daughter of Gilbert Frankau, the author. She wrote many popular novels. She was converted to Catholicism in 1942.

GREENAWAY, Kate (1846-1901). Painter and illustrator of children's books. Her style of drawing influenced many other artists and was much admired by Ruskin. She created a gallery of children in quaint costumes.

HENGLER, Frederick Charles (1820-87). A circus proprietor and owner of the Palais Royal, Argyll Street, London.

IRVING, Henry Brodribb (1870-1919). Actor and barrister. The elder son of Sir Henry Irving. His successes include Hamlet at the Adelphi, 1904, and *The Admirable Crichton* at the Duke of

York's, 1902-4. Also a writer on criminology.

KENSIT, John (1853-1902). Protestant agitator who started a Protestant book company in Paternoster Row. He was fatally wounded in a religious riot in Liverpool.

LISTER, Joseph, 1st Baron Lister of Lyme Regis (1827-1912). Originator of antiseptic surgery. He was Professor of Surgery at Glasgow Infirmary from 1861, and was much influenced by the researches of Louis Pasteur. He employed carbolic acid to kill germs.

LLOYD, Marie (1870-1922). originally Matilda Alice Victoria Wood. Musical comedy singer. She appeared in many music-halls in the East End, and gained fame with her studies in Cockney humour. She was married three times.

LONG, Edwin Longsden, R.A. (1829-91). Painter of many oriental subjects.

MAAS, Joseph (1847-86). Singer. He studied in Milan and performed in London at Drury Lane, and as principal tenor at Her Majesty's Theatre.

M'CARTHY, Justin (1830-1912). Irish writer and political reporter for the *Morning Star* and the *Daily News*. He entered Parliament in 1872, and is known principally for his works *The Four Georges* and *William IV*.

Charles Hengler

MACFARREN, Sir George Alexander (1813-87). Composer. He studied at the Royal Academy of Music, and became conductor at Covent Garden in 1845. His best-known works are *Symphony in C, The Devil's Opera* and an oratorio, *St John the Baptist.* His sight failed in 1860.

MARKS, Henry Stacy, R.A. (1829-98). Artist. At first he was employed in his father's coach-building business, painting heraldic devices on carriages. His early pictures were mainly humorous Shakespearean subjects, but in his later work he specialized in natural history subjects and seascapes. He exhibited at the Royal Academy from 1853, becoming a member in 1878. He was a member of the Society of Painters in Water-colours in 1883.

MICHAEL or Mikhail Mikhailovich, Grand Duke of Russia (1861-1929). He was exiled in 1891 because of his morganatic marriage with SOPHIE, Nikolaevna, Countess de Torry (1868-1927), who is also buried here.

O'BRIEN, Sir Tom (1900-1970). General Secretary of the National Association of Theatrical and Kine Employees. He started work as an errand boy, and became one of the great union leaders, travelling all over the world as a fraternal delegate, and twice President of the TUC.

PARKER, Rev Joseph (1830-1902). Of the City Temple. Congregationalist minister and orator. He visited America five times and published religious works.

PARRY, Joseph Haydn (1841c.-1903). Welsh composer of operettas, oratorios and anthems, and Professor at the Guildhall School of Music.

PEARSON, Sir Arthur, G.B.E. (1866-1921). President of the National Institute for the Blind and founder of the business, C. Arthur Pearson Ltd, of which he was chairman. He wrote books on blindness.

QUAIN, Sir Richard (1816-98). Physician in London from 1842 and Physician Extraordinary to Queen Victoria in 1890. He specialized in diseases of the chest. He was a Fellow of University College, London in 1842 and created a baronet of the United Kingdom in 1891.

QUARITCH, Bernard (1819-99). Bookseller. He was born in Prussian Saxony, but came to England and opened a business near Leicester Square and later in Piccadilly. He dealt in rare and foreign books.

TERRY, Fred (1863-1933). Actor. Brother of Ellen Terry. He made his debut at the Haymarket Theatre in 1880 and established his reputation as a romantic actor, playing many Shakespearean roles. He acted with Tree, Forbes Robertson and Irving. He was the father of Dennis and Phyllis Neilson-Terry. His wife, Julia NEILSON–TERRY, is also buried here.

SKETCH PLAN OF WEST HAMPSTEAD CEMETERY

FORTUNE GREEN ROAD

GATE

PUBLIC FOOTPATH

PUBLIC FOOTPATH

JEWISH BURIAL GROUND (BRADY ST)

1. BAYNES Thomas Spencer
2. BRAIN Dennis
3. COOPER Dame Gladys
4. FERRANTI Sebastian Ziani de
5. FISHER Andrew
6. FLETCHER Bannister
7. FRANKAU

8. GREENAWAY Kate
9. HENGLER Frederick Charles
10. KENSIT John
11. LISTER Joseph, 1st Baron Lister
    of Lyme Regis
12. LLOYD Marie

14. MARKS Henry Stacy
15. MICHAEL, Grand Duke of Russia
16. O'BRIEN Sir Tom
17. PEARSON Sir Arthur
18. QUAIN Sir Richard
19. TERRY Fred

BLOOMSBURY

Brunswick Square
CEMETERIES OF ST GEORGE AND ST GEORGE THE MARTYR

Underground: Russell Square

Buses: (to Russell Sq.), 68, 77

This was called Nelson's Burying Ground after Robert Nelson, the first person buried here. The cemeteries are now pleasant recreation grounds.

CAMPBELL, John (1708-55). Writer. The author of many histories and editor of *Biographia Britannica,* which was published in weekly parts. He was described by Boswell as 'the richest author that ever grazed the common of literature'.

CROMWELL, Anne (*c.* 1661-1727). The daughter of Richard Cromwell, third son of Oliver Cromwell.

CROMWELL, Mary (*c.* 1636-1712). Oliver Cromwell's daughter and sixth child.

Anne Cromwell

DAWSON, Nancy (*c.* 1730-1767). A famous hornpipe-dancer, and figure dancer at Sadlers Wells. She made her reputation by dancing the hornpipe in *The Beggar's Opera,* 1759.

LODGE, Edmund (1756-1839). Biographer. He was Bluemantle Pursuivant-at-Arms at the College of Arms, 1782. His chief work was a series of 'biographical and historical memoirs', 1821-34.

MACAULAY, Zachary (1768-1838). Philanthropist. He was manager of an estate in Jamaica, where he was shocked by the terrible miseries of the slave population. He later edited the *Christian Observer,* a periodical devoted to the abolition of the slave trade. He was governor of Sierra Leone, 1793-9.

MUNDEN, Joseph Shepherd (1758-1832). A leading actor with a company of strolling players, and the most celebrated comedian of his time. His acting ability was praised by Lamb, Hazlitt and Leigh Hunt.

NELSON, Robert (1665-1715). Religious writer and Fellow of the Royal Society, 1680. He took part in many acts of charity, especially for schools and parochial libraries. He was the author of *Festivals and Fasts.*

RICHARDSON, Jonathan, the Younger (1694-1771). Portrait painter. He followed the work of his father, who was himself successor to Kneller.

CAMDEN TOWN

Camden High Street   ST MARTIN'S GARDENS

Underground: Camden Town

Buses: 24, 29, 68

A small disused burial ground with a number of tombstones, some against the walls. Charles Dibdin's tomb and monument, erected by the Kentish Town Musical Society, is the only one of note that is visible.

DIBDIN, Charles (1744-1814). He composed music for Garrick, and was famous for his nautical songs. He also wrote a *History of the Stage*, 1795, and two novels.

HEWSON, Hugh (d. 1809). Said to be the original Hugh Strap in Smollett's *Roderick Random*.

PAYNE, Roger (1739-97). A famous bookbinder whose business was near Leicester Square.

ROOKER, Michael Angelo (1743-1801). Engraver and painter. He was a scene-painter at the Haymarket theatre and also exhibited water-colours at the Royal Academy.

Note: This churchyard belonged to St Martin-in-the-Fields.

Charles Dibdin

CHELSEA

Royal Hospital Road   HOSPITAL BURIAL GROUND

Buses: 11, 19, 22

This is a cemetery for Chelsea Pensioners and for people who have worked at the Royal Hospital.

BURNEY, Dr Charles (1726-1814). Musician and author who was the organist at the hospital. He was the author of *The General History of Music*. Father of Fanny Burney, (Madame D'Arblay) the novelist.

CHESELDEN, William (1688-1752). Surgeon at St Thomas's Hospital. He attended Sir Isaac Newton at his deathbed, and also invented the lateral operation for the stone, on which he published a treatise.

Two women who joined up as men in the army to search for their husbands: Christiana DAVIS and Hannah BELL. Only when they were wounded in the Crimean War was it discovered that they were female.

CHELSEA

Kings Road   MORAVIAN BURIAL GROUND

Buses: 11, 19, 22

Count Nikolaus Ludwig von Zinzendorf, leader of the Moravian movement in England, encouraged refugees from Bohemia and Moravia to settle on his estate at Chelsea.

GILLRAY, James (d. 1799). Father of the caricaturist, James Gillray. He was sexton here for forty years. He was a Lanark-man who fought in Flanders under the Duke of Cumberland, and lost an arm.

HUTTON, James (1715-95). A friend of Wesley. He broke with Wesley in 1740, and started the Moravian movement in England.

MARYLEBONE

Paddington Street   THE GARDENS

Underground: Baker Street

Buses: 2, 13, 26, 30, 74, 159

This was a burial ground, 1731-1857, but is now a pleasant garden, although still in the care of church authorities.

BARETTI, Giuseppe Marc Antonio (1719-89). Writer and compiler of an *Italian and English Dictionary*. He was a friend of Johnson. He was tried at the Old Bailey for killing a man who attacked him in the Haymarket, but was acquitted, 1769. His portrait was painted by Reynolds.

BONOMI, Joseph, the Elder (1734-1808). Architect. He was born in Rome but practised in London and exhibited drawings at the Royal Academy, 1783-1806. He worked mainly in the Grecian revival style.

GUTHRIE, William (1708-70). He wrote for the *Gentleman's Magazine* and was also author of *A General History of the World*, 1764-7.

STEPNEY   JEWISH BURIAL GROUNDS
Alderney Road, Mile End

Underground: Stepney Green

Bus: 25

Next to this burial ground there is a Spanish and Portuguese cemetery. This contains remains of the ancestors of Benjamin Disraeli, the Eardley family, Sampson Gideon and Ricardos Sapes, but the ground is due for clearance and the remains will be transferred to Brentwood.

HART, Moses (c. 1676-1756). Builder of the great synagogue at Aldgate in 1721, and brother of Aaron Hart, Chief Rabbi.

LEVI, David (1740-99). Jewish contro-versialist and a member of the London congregation of German and Polish

Jews. He was a shoemaker's apprentice. He acquired a good knowledge of Hebrew and in 1785 published *A* *Succinct Account of the Rites and Ceremonies of the Jews . . .* and also *A Defence of the Old Testament. . . .*

WHITECHAPEL

Brady Street, Whitechapel Road

Underground: Whitechapel

Buses: 25. 253

There was a Jewish burial ground at Cripplegate and Jewin Street was on this site. The cemeteries that are within easy reach, in the Whitechapel and Mile End areas, are all disused. Brady Street is the largest and has a rather interesting feature: according to Jewish rule, bodies should be buried one only to a grave, and no more than six feet from the surface of the ground. After about thirty years, when the Brady Street area was full, it was decided to put a four foot layer of earth on top of part of the ground and use this for more burials. This has resulted in a large flat-topped mound and it is perhaps the only cemetery where, because of the double layer, the headstones are placed back to back. To view these, permission has to be obtained from the United Synagogue.

HIRSCHEL, Solomon (1761-1842). Chief Rabbi of German and Polish Jews in London, 1802-42.

HURWITZ, Hyman (1770-1844). Professor of Hebrew at London University, 1828. Author of *Elements of the Hebrew Language,* a Hebrew grammar and poems. A friend of Coleridge.

LEVEY, Miriam (1801-56). Welfare worker who opened up the first soup kitchens for the poor in the Whitechapel area.

ROTHSCHILD, Nathan Meyer (1777-1836). Banker, money changer and dealer in curiosities. He established a business in London in 1805. His remains were brought from Germany, where he died, and buried here with those of his wife, Hannah (1783-1850).

Miriam Levey

BIBLIOGRAPHY

Clarke, Basil F. L., *Parish Churches of London,* Batsford, 1969
Cunningham, George H., *London,* Dent, 1927
Curll, Edmund, *The Inscriptions Upon The Tombs, Grave-Stones Etc., In The Dissenters Burial Place Near Bunhill Fields,* 1717
Curl, James Stevens, *The Victorian Celebration of Death,* David and Charles, 1972
Daniell, A. E., *London City Churches,* Constable, 1902
Ellen, R. G., *A London Steeplechase,* City Press, 1972
Gunnis, Robert, *Dictionary of British Sculptors 1660-1851,* Murray, 1951
Holmes, Isabella M., *The London Burial Grounds,* T. F. Unwin, 1896
Justyne, J. W., *Illustrated Guide to Highgate Cemetery,* 1865
　　　　　　　Illustrated Guide to Kensal Green Cemetery, 1858
Kent, William, *London For Everyman,* Dent, 1931, revised edition 1969
Stow, John, *The Survey of London,* Dent, 1912
Westminster Official Guide, 1965
Young, Elizabeth & Weyland, *Old London Churches,* Faber, 1956

INDEX

not
so

149

Villiers, Barbara, Countess of
Castlemaine and Duchess of
Cleveland, 74
Villiers, George, 62
Villiers, George, 1st Duke of
Buckingham, 64
Vincent, William, 61
Vivares, François, 88

Wade, George, 55
Wadloe, Simon, 26
Walbrook, Anton, 81
Waldby or Waldeby, Robert de, 62
Walker, John, 91
Waller, Sir William, 44
Walton, Rachel, 26
Walton (sons of Izaak Walton), 75
Walworth, Sir William, 32
Wanley, Humphrey, 87
Ward, James, 121
Ward, Dr Joshua, 60
Ward, Ned, 92
Warneford, Lieutenant, 129
Warner, Lucy, 72
Warren, Baron Sir William, 20
Watson, Thomas, 22
Watson, Musgrave Lewthwaite, 111
Watts, Alaric Alexander, 111
Watts, Isaac, 102
Webb, Sidney James, 1st Baron
Passfield, 56
Webbe, Samuel, 91
Webster, Benjamin Nottingham, 129
Wedgewood, Hensleigh, 80
Weever, John, 75
Welby, Henry, 27
Wellesley, Arthur, 1st Duke of
Wellington, 37
Wesley, Charles, 87
Wesley, John, 103
Wesley, Susannah, 102
West, Benjamin, 37
West (Jenny Diver), 80
Weston, Prior, 75
Wharton, Henry, 55
Wheatley, Francis, 87

Whistler, James Abott McNeill, 74
Whitefield, Elizabeth James, 82
Whitehead, George, 103
Whitehead, William, 44
Whittington, Richard, 31
Wilberforce, William, 57
Wilkes, John, 44
Wilkins, Dr John, 29
William III, Prince of Orange, 63
William Augustus, Duke of
Cumberland, 64
William, Duke of Gloucester, 63
William Windsor, 62
Williams, Daniel, 103
Williams, David, 45
Williams, Sir William Fenwick, 129
Wilson, Sir Henry Hughes, 37-8
Wingfield, Major Walter Clopton, 121
Winifred, Marchioness of Winchester, 62
Winwood, Sir Ralph, 22
Wiseman, Richard, 52
Wither or Withers, George, 53
Wombwell, George, 111
Wood, Ellen, 109
Wood, Sir Henry Joseph, 40
Woodfall, Henry Sampson, 73
Woodhead, Abraham, 91
Woodington, William Frederick, 133
Woodward, Dr John, 56
Woolston, Thomas, 92
Worde, Wynkyn de, 25
Worlidge, Thomas, 79
Wren, Sir Christopher, 38
Wriothesley, Sir Thomas, 1st Baron
Wriothesley of Titchfield and Earl
of Southampton, 21
Wyatt, James, 60
Wyatt, Mathew Cotes, 111
Wycherley, William, 52
Wymark, Patrick Carl, 109

Yates, Edmund, 111
Yevele, Henry de, 30

Zouche, Richard, 78

NOTES